DESIGNING AGENT   GY
AI THAT WORKS FOR PEOPLE

Christopher Noessel

Rosenfeld Media
Brooklyn, New York

Designing Agentive Technology

AI That Works for People

Christopher Noessel

Rosenfeld Media, LLC

540 President Street

Brooklyn, New York

11215 USA

On the Web: www.rosenfeldmedia.com

Please send errors to: errata@rosenfeldmedia.com

Publisher: Louis Rosenfeld

Managing Editor: Marta Justak

Illustrations: Nancy Januzzi and Christopher Noessel

Interior Layout: Danielle Foster

Cover Design: The Heads of State

Indexer: Marilyn Augst

Proofreader: Sue Boshers

ISBN-10: 1-933820-63-2

ISBN-13: 978-1-933820-63-7

LCCN: 2017934296

Printed and bound in the United States of America

This book is dedicated to my partner, Benjamin Remington, and our son, Miles. Thanks for your patience and inspiration as I spread mind maps over the dinner table, labored over outlines and sketches, nerded up dinner conversation, and tapped on keyboards into the wee hours. I love you both. Thank you for your support. When the Basilisk comes for us, we can present this book in our defense.

HOW TO USE THIS BOOK

Who Should Read This Book?

I have written this book with three (and a half) audiences in mind.

The first group is product owners and technology strategists, who will want to understand agentive technology as a strategic advantage and differentiator for their products. If this is you, you'll want to understand the value that agentive tech brings to your users and customers.

The second is interaction designers, educators, and students, who will want to have ways to talk about—and some ideas for kick-starting—their own projects that might involve agents. If this is you, understand the roots of these ideas (they go back far) and master the use cases and ethical questions involved.

The third is futurists and tech sector pundits, who might want to understand more of the opportunities that narrow artificial intelligence provides for people, organizations, and governments. If this is you, the model, examples, and speculative design ideas throughout the book should prove inspiring.

That "and a half" parenthetical is related to my work on scifiinterfaces.com, and that's for sci-fi makers. I can't tell you how many times I have been watching or reading sci-fi and found myself lamenting that the speculative designs in it are just *lame*. They haven't even caught up with current technology, much less painted a compelling vision of the future. So, hopefully, this will help writers and makers understand that technology can and should be doing some of the things their characters are. Sure, this will be a small sliver of my readership, but one that's near and dear to my nerdy heart. If this is you, understand what narrow AI can do, get ideas for your worldbuilding, and, of course, in the ethics section you can find ideas for dark new dystopias.

What's in This Book?

Despite solid advice to the contrary, I've structured this book as a logical argument because of the nature of the universe and who I am as a person.

Part I, "Seeing," makes the case for agentive technology, taking the stance that it's a genuinely new, unique, and exciting category of technology all on its own, with fascinating predecessors and deserving of its own consideration.

Part II, "Doing," presumes that you bought the argument presented in Part I, walking through use cases that are germane to the tech. The use cases are structured according to an explanatory model. To bring the use cases to life, I introduce a speculative gardening service called *Mr. McGregor*.

Part III, "Thinking," touches on what the consequences of the tech might be, including the future of the industry and the ethical questions that this technology raises. It's not light summer reading fare. It's not meant to be.

To make the book easily referenced, **Appendix A, "Consolidated Touchpoints,"** brings together all the use cases into a single place. There, they are first presented chronologically, and then according to the conceptual model used to introduce the chapters in Part II.

Appendix B, "A List of Referenced Agentive Technology," collects the real-world examples mentioned in the course of the text. There are other agentive technologies out there, and I expect there will be many more in the future. But if you're trying to remember that one "chaperone" service, you should be able to find it there more quickly.

What Comes with This Book?

This book has a companion website (http://rosenfeldmedia.com/books/designing-agentive-technology/). The book's diagrams and other illustrations are available under a Creative Commons license (when possible) for you to download and include in your own presentations. If you do so, please make sure to credit Rosenfeld Media, Christopher Noessel, and the copyright owner, if it is separate. You can find these illustrations on Flickr at www.flickr.com/photos/rosenfeldmedia/sets/. Additionally, the author keeps tweeting on this topic as @AgentiveTech and will try to keep new material at agentive.ai, including speaking engagements and opportunities.

FREQUENTLY ASKED QUESTIONS

How do you pronounce "agentive"?

"Agentive" is a once-languishing adjective that is built on the word "agent," so I pronounce it emphasizing the first syllable, "Ā-jen-tiv." I like that this pronunciation points back to its root, which helps people suss out its meaning when they're hearing it for the first time. I've heard people stress the second syllable, as "uh-**JEN**-tiv," which rolls off the tongue just fine, but doesn't do much to help people's understanding.

Did you invent this kind of technology?

Oh no, far from it. As you'll read in Chapter 4, "Six Takeaways from the History of Agentive Thinking," thoughts about machines that take some sort of initiative go all the way back to at least ancient Greece. So, no, I didn't invent it. I have designed several agentive systems over the past few years, though, and on about my third such project, realized I was seeing some recurring patterns (in the Christopher Alexander sense). I looked for a book on a user-centered approach to this kind of technology, and when I could not find one, decided to write it.

What's the most accessible example of agentive technology you can give me?

Chapter 1, "The Thermostat That Evolved," goes into some detail on one example that is popular in the United States, the Nest Thermostat. If you're not in the U.S., or unfamiliar with that product, imagine an automatic pet feeder. It is not a tool for you to feed your cat. It has tools for you to specify how you want *the machine* to feed your cat, and the feeder does most of the rest. You will still need to refill it, free food stuck in its rotors, and occasionally customize or pause feeding schedules. These maintenance and customization touchpoints are what distinguishes it from *automation* and where design plays a major role. To flesh out this singular example, see Appendix B for a list of every other real-world example included in the book.

I have an agentive project beginning. How can you help me start it out right?

Begin with the first diagram shown in Appendix A, "Consolidated Touchpoints." It shows common use cases in a rough, chronological order. Think through your product and identify which use cases apply to your project and which don't. Reference the chapters in Part II for details on the use cases and begin to construct scenarios around them. This should give you a great head start.

Why didn't you go into depth about interfaces?

Agentive technology differs primarily in *use cases*, rather than interfaces, so Part II is dedicated to identifying and describing these. Readers can draw on the existing practices of interaction and interface design for best practices around individual touchpoints. The notable exception is the interface by which a user specifies triggers and behaviors. See Chapter 5, "A Modified Frame for Interaction" for an introduction to these concepts, and Chapter 8, "Handling Exceptions," for an interface pattern called a "Constrained Natural Language Builder," which you can consider customizing in your agentive interfaces.

You're just another cheerleader for the future, blithely bringing artificial intelligence doom down on us all! Wake up, sheeple!

Technically, that's not a question, and frankly a little hyperbolic. But I'm still here to help. There's a distinction to learn in Chapter 2, *"Fait Accompli:* Agentive Tech Is Here," between narrow artificial intelligence and general artificial intelligence. Once you understand that difference, it becomes easier to understand that, unlike general AI, narrow AI gets safer as it gets smarter. And as you'll read at the end of Chapter 12, "Utopia, Dystopia, and Cat Videos," I believe a worldwide body of agentive rules is a useful data set to hand to a general AI if/when one comes online, to help it understand how humans like to be treated. This is on the good side of the fight.

Aren't you that sci-fi interfaces guy?

I am one of them. I keep the blog scifiinterfaces.com, and you may have heard me speaking on the topic, attended a workshop, or been to one of my sci-fi movie nights. Also, Nathan Shedroff and I co-authored *Make It So: Interaction Design Lessons from Science Fiction* in 2012, which is all about what real-world designers can learn from speculative interfaces. Predictably, sci-fi makes appearances in this book. You'll see some quick mentions in Chapter 2, and two important mentions in Chapter 13, "Your Mission, Should You Choose to Accept It." These serve as a telling contrast of sci-fi written with and without agentive concepts. You also can search the #agentive tag on the scifiinterfaces.com blog to find even more.

If you could wave your hands and make anything an agent, what would it be?

Well, I must admit that part of the reason I chose Mr. McGregor to be the illustrative example is that I grew up in big cities, far from farmsteads, and never got the knack of raising plants. If, like me, you have a brown thumb, but dream of growing your own garden-fresh food, read about Mr. McGregor in sections placed after Chapters 5, 6, 7, and 8. My second choice might be an agent on mobile phones that listens in on conversations and does some socially adept fact-checking and frame-checking to encourage skeptical thinking and discourage lies or bullshit, in the H. G. Frankfurt sense.

CONTENTS

CHAPTER 4

Six Takeaways from the History
of Agentive Thinking

PART II: DOING

CHAPTER 5

A Modified Frame for Interaction

FOREWORD

Chris has written a surprising book. He's written something so inherently human that you can't help but be swept up into the new world of agentive technology. To be honest, it's just not fair! It sneaks up on you because Chris effortlessly shows the progression toward agentive technology—toward our giving agency to *technology*—to be simply an obvious step in *human* evolution. That's a profound, and useful, shift of mindset.

Chris tells the story of *artificial* intelligence from the perspective of *human* imagination (sci-fi, scary) and of *technical* capabilities from the perspective of *human* needs and desires (real, narrow, beneficial). It's a sleight of hand that brings perspective to some of the "sky is falling" noise that's out there right now around AI. More importantly, this approach makes it all so relatable (and, yes, readable). You won't leave here knowing how machines learn, but you will appreciate better how machine learning might impact the humans who rely on it. You'll also be introduced to the implications of that reliance over time. These might surprise you—it's not about AI as a sinister overlord, but rather the seemingly mundane implications of a machine's lack of empathy.

Again, humanity. I'm so struck with how human this book is.

It's a book about invention and the evolution of ideas, technologies, and desires. I think maybe the single biggest trick Chris performs here is that by providing the history of various tools and their creators (like temperature control technology), the obviousness of technical assistants is almost shown to be a refined human need, as opposed to a new technical capability. This completely changes how we should approach the design of agents. It argues for, well, human-centered design, now, doesn't it?

And that, finally, is what leaps from these pages: the need for new practices in human-centered design. Without approaching the problem from a "framework" perspective (thank you), Chris offers the first word on some of these practices. He adds depth to the understanding of how agents differ from tools (both hardware and software). And by covering agentive technology's human impacts, he shows that industrial design, UX design, and service design don't adequately address what's required to understand and solve problems of agentive technologies.

This is just the beginning of a new conversation in design, for sure, but wow—what a great start!

Phil Gilbert
General Manager, Design
IBM Corporation
March 22, 2017

INTRODUCTION

Thanks for picking this book up to give it a read. But, seriously—how do you have the time?

I look at my should-read book stack and at the precious minutes of free-choice time I have, and I'm dismayed. With a little research, I find that there are around 1,500 books published in my mother tongue around the world *every day*. That's one every 57.6 seconds. Even if only one in 10,000 of them is truly amazing, that means there's a new one to add to the stack *each week*. There's just no way to keep up.

It's not just reading. We're all under pressure to do more and more with the time we have. If it's not an existential bony finger reminding us to *carpe* every *diem*, it's just the nature of the world to tell you that you should be doing more. You should be flossing more, bonding with your sweetheart and children more, and taking longer to eat your meal that you should have homegrown and cooked yourself. You should be looking at your finances more, meditating more, getting outside and exercising more. Sleeping more.

If you look at actual studies like the annual American Time Use Survey by the U.S. Bureau of Labor Statistics, there's not a lot of wiggle room in our schedules. If you're one of their mythical average Americans, you dedicate all of 16—*count-em*—16 minutes of time to relax and think each day.[1] Even if you try to carve time away from the optional activities like television and movies, it's quite likely some of the non-optional activities like sleeping and household chores could easily expand to consume the excess.

External time pressures aren't going away, and I doubt we're going to lose the internal desire to maximize the precious little time we have.

Enter technology.

---

1 Here I'm referencing the 2008 data set, if only because the *New York Times* illustrated it so brilliantly. And apologies for not having more global studies to cite. I don't mean to be this culture-specific.

For decades, technology has helped us move faster. It used to take hours to get furniture off a carpet and then take the carpet outside, drape it over something, and beat it clean. The vacuum cleaner shrank that to minutes. It's part of the point of this book to show that lately, some technological innovations are shrinking that time to nearly zero. Consider the Roomba and what it means to get back those minutes of time you used to spend beating your rugs clean. These technologies aren't just *helping* you do things. They've begun to do things *for you*. And as you'll see, faster isn't the only benefit that these agentive technologies provide.

That's an exciting development, but to the best of my knowledge, it's happening in a haphazard way—product strategists, owners, designers, and developers doing smart work in their own organizational silos. But could we do it better if we got clear on what we're talking about? Say if we took a big, broad look at what makes these things special and unique and saw what patterns and problems emerged? That's what this book is about.

So thanks for making the time. I think what you invest here, and the technology that results with this new thinking, is going to make the future a brighter place.

PART I

Seeing

In the first part of this book, I hope to do something that is not only arrogant but also damned difficult. I hope to change the way you look at technology. First, I want you to stop seeing it as a collection of tools or gadgets and instead see it as an evolutionary flow around human problems, whose parts ultimately integrate to become a new category of thing.

To help you see it this way, we'll start by looking at the rich example of the thermostat and how it evolved from the past to the present. Then I'll show you that this example isn't some special, isolated case. Rather, once you know to look for it, you can tell that it's just on the verge of happening pretty much everywhere else. Then we'll move our focus from the present into the speculative future to see how this new category of technology will change the world.

We'll finish Part I by looking at lines of thought that have in the past intersected with this concept. In Part II, "Doing," we'll start to make use of this new approach to design smarter products. But for now, let's jump in and talk about dinosaurs.

The Thermostat That Evolved

Let's begin with an evolutionary fable. About 275 million years ago, a tiny, lizard-like creature broke free from its egg with a trait that was very unusual for its kind. Unlike the rest of her cold-blooded family, whose body temperature matched the ambient temperature, this little mutant produced her own heat. On the positive side, her mutation meant she could move around just fine in winter while her kin slowed down. On the negative side, it meant that she was ravenous all the time, and could feel cold and heat as direct threats to her weird new metabolism. To compensate, she had to develop some adaptive behaviors—that is, she had to find ways to stay cool in summers and warm in winters.

Fast-forward the video of this tale, and despite her being a world-class weirdo, she thrives and has kids. Her kids have kids. Two hundred million years pass and what was like a thick lizard now looks more like early platypuses, kangaroos, and mice. Cold-blooded types eyeball them suspiciously over mouthfuls of weird Cretaceous insects. Then, out of nowhere, a cataclysmic asteroid drops. Cold-blooded creatures cannot handle the global climate change like the mutant ones do. Goodbye dinosaurs, hello vacant ecological niche. After the dust clears: more kids, who dutifully evolve and speciate. Tree climbers. Grass eaters. Sea swimmers. Primates. Homo Sapiens. "Hello world!" Then ultimately, *you*, wherever you are, reading this book. Most of which can be traced back to that tiny therapsid's weird mutation.

This is an oversimplified (seriously, don't base your paleontology degree on this) introduction to the mammalian branch of the tree of life. We're a small part of that branch, and it means we're stuck with those same positives and negatives of being homeothermic, notably that we have to work to keep ourselves comfortable—neither too cold nor too warm. There are behaviors, of course, like huddling together or staying in shadow, but this book is about the evolution of tools. So what tools have we used to help us with the warm-blooded problem of temperature regulation?

Tools for Temperature

Grab a broad leaf with a sturdy stem, and you'll have a simple fan to move air around. Wrap yourself in fur, blanket, or cloth and you can keep more of your body heat on you. Find a branch struck by lightning and you can carry that flame around, set the flammable stuff alight (whee!), and put the fire inside spaces, which can contain that heat.

Fireplaces, furnaces, and furnace doors allow some manual control of warm air. Even architectural features like curtains, doors, and windows act as simple tools that help control the flow of air, keeping the comfortable air on you and the uncomfortable air at bay.

These tools allowed you to physically work to control the temperature. That was on top of all of the labor required by the rest of living. Sometimes it was too much. (Get up and bar the door!) Such was the poor state of human thermal management until the Mennonites brought us a Dutch inventor by the name of Cornelis Drebbel.

Drebbel's Incubator

Born in Alkmaar, North Holland in 1572, Drebbel was the fair-haired, handsome son of a landowner (or farmer, history is vague on the details).[1] At an early age, he was sent to apprentice under the engraver Hendrick Goltzius, whose interest in alchemy rubbed off on the young pupil. Alkmaar at the time was also home to a large group of Mennonite

COURTESY OF WIKIMEDIA COMMONS

1 www.encyclopedia.com/topic/Cornelis_ Jacobszoon_Drebbel.aspx

scientists and inventors, and Cornelis' young mind showed both an interest in and aptitude for invention. In his mid-to-late 20s, he was granted patents for a pump, a "perpetual motion" clock, and a chimney design. After marrying Feijtge, one of the younger sisters of his master (hey, a young apprentice can't be expected to engrave *all* the time), he moved to seek greater fortunes in London. There his inventions caught the attention of King James I, and he was invited into the service of Henry, Prince of Wales, where he worked on other inventions. Despite a brief stint at court in Prague, it was in England that Cornelis lived out his days and invented what is regarded as the first automatic temperature regulator.

It worked like this: Inside an oven, furnace, or incubator, the warming air would cause a column of mercury to slowly rise until it would close a damper on the heat source. This closure allowed the temperature to drop back down slowly, lowering the mercury and reopening the damper. The simple feedback mechanism allowed Drebbel to tweak the height of the column of mercury and the qualities of the damper to gain fairly good automatic control over the temperature.

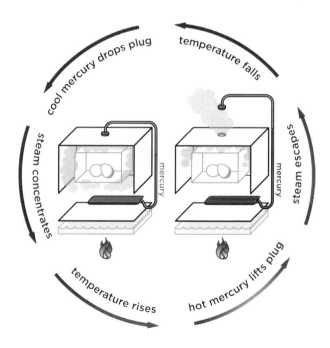

For the first time, people didn't need to put in manual effort to manage the specific warmth of a space. What is now known as a *feedback loop* inside the machine managed it all for them automatically. It was a lot less work. Using the Drebbel system, people didn't need to use a tool, but could just set up a heat source and leave it running until they no longer wanted the heat.

Others would later invent competing mechanisms, but they were still its conceptual heirs.

In 1885, Albert Butz was granted a patent on a device with the ungainly name of "damper flapper," which lifted a flap as it got cold, fueling a fire with more air, and lowering again as it heated up. That patent gained the attention of a young engineer named Mark Honeywell, who purchased it and 20 years later under the auspices of the Electric Heat Regulator Company released the Jewell thermostat to the market. It included a thermometer to add some objective data to the temperature-setting task.

Around the same time, Warren S. Johnson used pneumatics in the late 1880s to allow for automatic temperature control in individual rooms. His product formed the basis of Johnson Controls, which has since evolved into the megacorporation Johnson & Johnson.

The invention of electricity allowed engineers in the 1950s to replace clunky analog components with tidier wires and circuits. In that same decade, Henry Dreyfuss, working for the now-giant Honeywell corporation, introduced the Round, a gorgeously designed thermostat that combined the thermometer readout with the control wheel in a unified way. It was not only an icon of gorgeous mid-century modern design, but it was also *the* thermostat control in most homes for nearly three decades.

In the 1980s, the Round[2] was displaced by cheaper molded plastic boxes, and its electrical wiring was replaced with computer circuitry, making thermostats cheaper to produce and their electronic insides more durable. A few thermostats introduced the option to connect an air conditioner as well, giving the user a switch that shifted from a HEAT mode for winter to a COOL mode for summer. A precious few enabled you to set hot and cold limits in a single control. But despite these improvements, for our purposes, each of these changes was incremental. It wasn't until well after the Age of Computers that thermostats made another major leap in evolution.

But before we get there, let me make a last appreciative shout-out to Cornelis, who, by the way, also invented revolutionary new dyeing techniques, the first submarine, a solar-powered harpsichord, and magic lantern devices. He furthered the field of optics and wrote a treatise on alchemy that would remain popular and in print for 100 years. Sadly owing to the capricious attentions of the royal court, the unlucky fellow died poor. His peers Kepler and Galileo are revered as historical geniuses, but Drebbel is a footnote with the occasional historian's nod. We did name a crater on the moon for you, Cornelis. It's the least we could do for centuries of your legacy.

---

2 If you want to learn more about Dreyfuss and the Round, read Alexandra Lange's article "Reinventing the Thermostat" from 2011 in The Design Observer. Also watch the Coen Brother's hilarious movie, *The Hudsucker Proxy,* as the character Norville Barnes seems to be inspired by Dreyfuss' famous circles. You know, for kids.

Then the Nest Learning Thermostat

That aforementioned leap of thermostat evolution is, of course, the Nest Learning Thermostat. Let's look at how the Nest Thermostat is different than what came before it.

COURTESY OF NEST LABS

Even with feedback control mechanisms on older thermostats allowing people to set the temperature thresholds that suited them best, those "dumb" thermostats still had to have their thresholds adjusted to account for personal tastes, time of day, humidity, and the seasons. In contrast, the Nest Thermostat connects to the home network to know the home's location and the calendar date. It knows the humidity and current weather. It knows how long it takes to change your home's temperature. It has smart defaults such that most people can just hook it up and let it run. But when homeowners find themselves uncomfortable at any time and adjust the temperature, the Nest Learning Thermostat pays attention to the change. It regards it as input. It learns. *OK*, its algorithm thinks, *this family likes it a little cooler in spring. Got it. I'll remember that for next spring.* (And its memory is perfect.)

Power users of the device can set up schedules that save on energy usage, either while they are routinely away at work and school, or for ad-hoc times like vacations and business trips. It talks to and coordinates with their carbon monoxide alarm and outdoor cameras. Rich feedback mechanisms, piped to smartphones and websites, help users visualize energy consumption and engage both ecological and competitive sensibilities to encourage saving money and energy.

The Nest Thermostat is still evolving as a product and refining its ability to deliver on its promise, but let's take a moment to consider how far the concept of the thermostat has come.

Recap: From Tool to Agent

The palm frond and fan are tools that let you cool yourself. Drebbel's incubator was a system that let you set a threshold to run against until further notice. The Nest Thermostat acts as a personal temperature regulator. It is as if you had hired a wise and happy butler to stand there at the thermostat, using everything that he knows about the clock, public and personal calendars, as well as the general preferences and statuses of the people in the house, to help them effortlessly achieve that persistent challenge that was bestowed upon them by *Tetraceratops insignis* eons ago—to keep themselves at a comfortable temperature. Even if its best guess is wrong, it's happy to adjust to your request—and moreover to remember. That is a thermostat that has evolved.

This remarkable evolution is happening not just to thermostats, but to almost every device and service that you use. As you'll see in the next chapter, tools are becoming agentive.

CHAPTER 2

Fait Accompli: Agentive Tech Is Here

In the prior chapter, we followed temperature control technology from its evolutionary origins through several stages—from the moment our distant forebears developed the need to control their temperature by behavior to using handheld fans and windows, and from the invention of the automated thermostat to the Nest Thermostat.

Tracing this journey is important because it is not unique to thermostats. These increasingly sophisticated technological solutions to the broad general problem of human temperature management illustrate two points. The first is that the evolution of tools can be viewed as iterated solutions to some core human need. The second is that agents are a natural solution to a great many computable human problems, as designers attempt to reduce effort and maximize results.

In this chapter, I'll define what an agent *is* and *is not*, use the thermostat as an example of one, look at some other technologies through a similar lens, and then make the case that far from being a sci-fi future, agents are beginning to appear in the world around us. They're not yet ubiquitous, but it's easy to see how they will be.

To start, let's go back and look at the temperature management tools. But this time, let's ask what work they are doing on behalf of the user.

Reducing Physical Work

The first and most obvious work that tools can do is to simplify and abstract the physical work involved in a task.

Early tools, like the handheld fan, are tools that simply shape the physical forces that the user is applying to them. The fan spreads out force over a plane, moving air more effectively than we could with our hand alone. These kinds of tools help save us work by letting us use materials and forms better suited to the task than our body parts. A fan is much better at moving air than our outspread hand is. Most technologies start their lives as these manual tools.

Tools can begin to take on the physical effort for us as well, by harnessing forces other than human muscles. Mills let us harness wind- and waterpower. Yokes let us harness animal power. The damper-flapper mechanism that Albert Butz invented saved us from having to get up and cross the room to open a furnace door, by harnessing electricity. These powered tools turn us from laborers to task-managers, steering and guiding the forces to do useful work.

Reducing Information Work

In addition to labor, technology can also help us with the information work involved in a task.

Of course, thermometers give a user some facts to work with in managing the heat of a space.

> What's the actual temperature here? Is it just me who's feeling cold? What temperature is the thermostat set to? Is it currently putting out heat or not? Is it even on?

These metrical tools give us facts to help us make decisions while performing a task.

More sophisticated technologies can begin to understand the rules of how a task should be performed, and let the user know when good form is being violated or thresholds crossed. These corrective tools help them understand what's going on and correct course if they're off track. If a user sets a thermometer to a temperature higher than it could actually attain, for instance, it could immediately provide this feedback and suggest additional measures that could be taken. This would be corrective.

Putting Physical and Information Work Together to Become Agentive

It's when someone takes these two things—information awareness and machines doing physical work—and connects the two that you begin to see some magic happen. That's when the tools become *agentive*.

Drebbel's incubator was the first tool to do this. It took in information about the temperature to open and close the damper. As brilliant as it was for its time, it was still something of a dumb temperature monitor. It only paid attention to a single variable, and only acted when that variable went above an amount. It couldn't help if the eggs were getting close to freezing. It didn't help the alchemist know when fuel was running low. You can consider this an agent, but just barely.

The Nest Thermostat is a much more complicated actor, able to track and manage many variables at once. It even learns over time, refining its model of what good behavior means in its particular household, on this particular day, and for the people it knows are currently present. It is a very powerful tool for managing temperature, and much more exemplary of what you can think of as an agent today.

The thing is, you can examine the history of technology solutions around a human need and find similar patterns. Tools will start out manual. Some evolve to reduce physical effort and become powered. Others evolve to help with the information work and become metrical for measuring or assistive for staying within known rules. And of late, you can see a few dozen examples of systems combining the information and the physical work to do work on behalf of its users, becoming agentive. That these patterns repeat across history is a big claim, but let's use three examples to illustrate: writing, music, and search.

The Problem of Writing

The Paleolithic cave paintings at Lascaux illustrate an ancient human need of mark-making. This evolution splits in two directions. One is toward expression, like paint brushes, but let's follow the other direction that veers toward writing. Around this human need, manual tools include burnt sticks, graphite pencils, and pens. There's not much physical effort involved in writing, but typewriters, both manual and electric, are powered tools that let people output many more letters per minute with less muscle fatigue and much more precision to the letterforms.

In addition, the advent of background spelling and grammar checkers on computers provide both metrical and assistive tools to keep you within the many conventions for clear writing. They've now evolved from simple rule-checkers like Sector Software's Spellbound to more sophisticated ones like Microsoft Word's grammar checker and iOS AutoCorrect, which not only notes misspellings, but immediately corrects the ones in which it has a high degree of confidence. Recently, Google Inbox released its Smart Reply, which parses incoming emails and provides several short, likely responses from which the user can simply select.

It all becomes agentive with the introduction of x.ai. Subscribers to this meeting scheduler only need to CC "Amy Ingram" (we see what you did there, x.) in an email asking her to "find us a time to meet" and "she" handles the rest. If you prefer a dude, the agent is happy to go by Alex as well. X.ai finds good times in your calendar, suggests them to the other people, works through conflicts, and lets you know when a fitting time has been found and a calendar reminder has been added to your calendar.

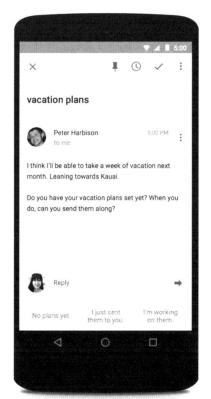

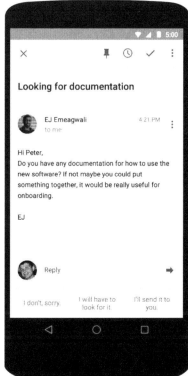

The Problem of Music Playback

Musical notation permitted the "recording" of music onto vellum, parchment, and paper, which could be played back with the manual tool of an instrument like a guitar or piano and let the human do all the decrypting work of turning those dots and lines into sound. The invention of powered tools like gramophones and record players let anyone hear a recording of a particular performance—you just had to manage collecting the music and switching out the disk yourself. CD players were also powered tools for playing, but being electronic first added metrical data like track numbers and later included artists and song titles to the display. (There are very few *rules* to how the user plays music, so you wouldn't expect to see any corrective technologies, though if you looked at equalizer controls there would be certain thresholds to be managed via a spectrum analyzer.) Radio stations have for a long time had disc jockeys act as a service for selecting and broadcasting music, but more recently Pandora and

Spotify are popular services with agentive aspects that let individual music listeners provide the system with a song or two they do like, and thereafter just listen.

  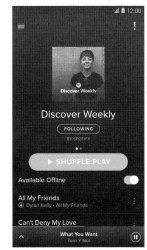

The Problem of Search

Search might seem like an odd example, since at first it seems just like information, but then you realize how much physical work used to be involved in finding information even in a well indexed system. Card catalogs were an early manual technology for providing search-like access to the information spread out in space in the stacks of a library. Microfiche is a powered system for reducing the amount of effort in looking through periodicals. Modern automated retrieval systems are powered tools that even bring a particular book to you on request. Metrical tools like tables of contents and indexes help you jump to particular parts of content.

However, once information exploded on the internet, Yahoo!, Google, Bing, and its ilk made the task of searching easier, and even helped you with corrective tools when you misspelled something, or when you were using poor search terms. *Did you mean . . .?* When Google introduced Google Alerts, it introduced low-level agents by which users could set up topics of interest and let the information come find them.

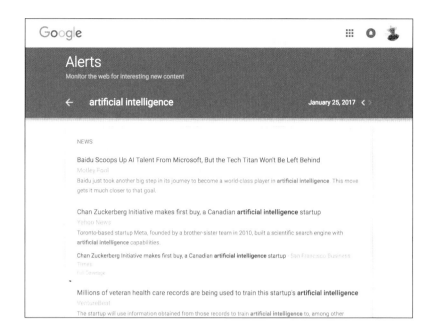

So that's just three examples. I'll cover many more in the next chapter and throughout the rest of the book. These three are, of course, cherry-picked from the vast history of technology, but should help to illustrate how these lenses are a useful way to understand the ways that various technologies have worked to reduce effort around particular human problems in categorical ways, and how very recent technologies combine these aspects into agents.

Getting to a Working Definition of "Agentive"

So between the Nest Thermostat in the prior chapter and the handful just covered, you've seen some examples of agentive technology, but rather than relying on inference, let's get specific about what an agent is and isn't.

> In the simplest definition, an agent is a piece of narrow artificial intelligence that acts on behalf of its user.

Looking at each aspect of that definition will help you understand it more fully. First, let's take the notion of narrow intelligence, and then acting on behalf of its user.

The Notion of Narrow Artificial Intelligence

When most people think of AI, they think of what they see in the movies. Maybe you imagine BB-8 rolling along the sands of Jakku, werping and wooing as it trails Rey. If you know a bit of sci-fi history you might also have a black-and-white robot in mind, like Gort or Robbie, policing or protecting per their job description. Or maybe you realize that AI doesn't need to be embodied in robot form, as with Samantha, the disembodied "operating system" OS1 in the movie *Her*—one minute sorting her user's inbox, the next falling in love with and then abandoning him. Or if you have an affinity for the darker side of things, you might think of either HAL's glowing red eye or MU/TH/R 6000's cold, screen-green text, each AI assaulting its crew members to protect their secret missions.

These sci-fi AIs—and, in fact, the overwhelming majority of sci-fi AIs—fall into three categories of *strong* artificial intelligence.

The first is the most advanced category of strong AI, which is called *artificial super intelligence*, and describes an AI with capabilities advanced far beyond human capabilities, and far beyond what you can even imagine. As a bird's intelligence is to human intelligence, a human intelligence is to ASI. As the scenario goes, if you program AGIs to evolve or make better and better copies of themselves, it will result in ever-accelerating improvements until they achieve what you can only call a godlike intelligence. Samantha from *Her* is a good sci-fi example, who by the end of the movie is accessing and contributing to the total body of human endeavor, having simultaneous conversations and relationships with users and other AIs, all while evolving to such a degree that she and the other AIs ultimately decide to leave humans behind as they sort of self-rapture to something or somewhere incomprehensible to humans.

The second is *artificial general intelligence*, or AGI, so called because it displays a general or abstract problem-solving capability similar to a human intelligence. BB-8 and HAL are examples of this. They are artificial, but are fairly human in their capabilities. They're one of the team. If/when we ever get to this, we'll be in a categorically different place than agentive tech.

The third category is "weak" or *artificial narrow intelligence*, or ANI. This is much more constrained AI, which might be fantastic at, say, searching a massive database of tens of millions of songs for a new one you're likely to love, but is still unable to play a game of tic-tac-toe. The intelligence these systems display cannot generalize, cannot of its own accord apply what it "knows" to new categories of problems. It's the AI that is in the world today, so familiar that you don't think of it as AI as much as you think of it simply as smart technology.

Whether or when we actually get to strong AGI is a matter for computer scientists, but for the purposes of design, it is immaterial. If AGI ever makes it to your Nest Thermostat, it will be making decisions about how best to use its resources to manage its task and communicate with its users, that is, to create its own interface and experience. Designers will not be specifying such systems as much as acting as consultants to the early AGIs on best practices. But until we've got AGI around to worry about, we have increasing numbers of examples of products and services built around ANI, and those will need good design to make them humane and useful.

As you saw in the prior examples, narrow intelligence isn't a binary quality. Different agents can embody different levels of intelligence. An agent can be said to be more intelligent when it has the following characteristics:

- **Its model of its domain is more reticulated and closer to our own.** Anyone who has been plunged into darkness by spending "too much" time in a restroom with a motion-sensing light switch knows that it is less smart than one that could "see" when there is a human there who still needs the light.

- **It successfully monitors more—and more complex—data streams.** Drebbel's device monitored a single variable, but the Nest Thermostat monitors dozens.

- **It can make smart inferences.** It can smartly infer what given data means and react accordingly. Steady weight gain over the course of the month might mean a homecare patient's sedentary choices may be increasing their body mass index. But rapid weight gain can mean dangerous swelling in the tissues—signs of a more serious medical concern.

- **It can plan.** This means considering multiple options for achieving a goal, taking into account the trade-offs between them, and selecting the best one.

- **It is adaptable**. It's able to use feedback to track its progress toward its goal and adjust its plans accordingly.

- **In advanced agents, this can mean the capability to refine predictive models with increasing experience and as new real-time information comes in.** Called *machine learning* in the vernacular, this helps narrow AIs adapt to an individual's behavior and get better over time. I'll touch on machine learning a bit more later, but for now understand that software can be programmed to make itself better at what it does over time.

So agents are properly defined as artificial *narrow* intelligence—AI that is strictly fit to one domain. But where ANI is a category, the agent is the instance, the thing that will act on behalf of those users. So let's talk about that second aspect of the definition.

Acting on Behalf of Its User

Similar to intelligence, agency can be thought of as a spectrum. Some things are more agentive than others. Is a hammer agentive? No. I mean if you want to be indulgently philosophical, you could propose that the metal head is acting on the nail per request by the rich gestural command the user provides to the handle. But the fact that it's always available to the user's hand during the task means it's a tool—that is, part of the user's attention and ongoing effort.

Less philosophically, is an internet search an example of an agent? Certainly the user states a need, and the software rummages through its internal model of the internet to retrieve likely matches. This direct cause-and-effect means that it's more like the hammer with its practically instantaneous cause-and-effect. Still a tool.

But as you saw before, when Google lets you save that search, such that it sits out there, letting you pay attention to other things, and lets you know when new results come in, now you're talking about something that is much more clearly acting on *behalf* of its user in a way that is distinct from a tool. It handles tasks so that you can use your limited attention on something else. So this part of "acting on your behalf"—that it does its thing while out of sight and out of mind—is foundational to the notion of what an agent is, why it's new, and why it's valuable. It can help you track something you would find tedious, like a particular moment in time, or a special kind of activity on the internet, or security events on a computer network.

To do any of that, an agent must monitor some stream of data. It could be something as simple as the date and time, or a temperature reading from a thermometer, or it could be something unbelievably complicated, like watching for changes in the contents of the internet. It could be data that is continuous, like wind speed, or irregular, like incoming photos. As it watches this data stream, it looks for triggers and then runs over some rules and exceptions to determine if and how it should act. Most agents work indefinitely, although they could be set to run for a particular length of time or when any other condition is met. Some agents like a spam filter will just keep doing their job quietly in the background. Others will keep going until they need your attention, and some will need to tell you right away. Nearly all will let you monitor them and the data stream, so you can check up on how they're doing and see if you need to adjust your instructions.

So those are the basics. Agentive technology watches a data stream for triggers and then responds with narrow artificial intelligence to help its user accomplish some goal. In a phrase, it's a persistent, background assistant.

If those are the basics, there are a few advanced features that a sophisticated agent might have. It might infer what you want without your having to tell it explicitly. It might adapt machine learning methods to refine its predictive models. It might gently fade away in smart ways such that the user gains competence. You'll learn about these in Part II, "Doing," of this book, but for now it's enough to know that agents can be much smarter than the basic definition we've established here.

How *Different* Are Agents?

Since most of the design and development process has been built around building good tools, it's instructive to compare and contrast them to good agents—because they are different in significant ways.

One of the main assertions of this book is that these differences are enough to warrant different ways of thinking about, planning for, and designing technology. They imply new use cases to master and new questions for evaluating them. They call for a community of practitioners to form around them.

TABLE 2.1 COMPARING MENTAL MODELS

A Tool-Based Model	An Agent-Based Model
A good tool lets you do a task well.	A good agent does a task for you per your preferences.
A hammer might be the canonical model.	A valet might be the canonical model.
Design must focus on having strong affordances and real-time feedback.	Design must focus on easy setup and informative touchpoints.
When it's working, it's ready-to-hand, part of the body almost unconsciously doing its thing.	When the agent is working, it's out of sight. When a user must engage its touchpoints, they require conscious attention and consideration.
The goal of the designer is often to get the user into *flow* (in the Mihalyi Csikszentmihalyi sense) while performing a task.	The goal of the designer is to ensure that the touchpoints are clear and actionable, to help the user keep the agent on track.

Drawing a Boundary Around Agentive Technology

To make a concept clear, you need to assert a definition, give examples, and then describe its boundaries. Some things will not be worth considering because they are obviously *in*; some things will not be worth considering because they are obviously *out*; but the interesting stuff is *at the boundary*, where it's not quite clear. What is on the edge of the concept, but specifically isn't the thing? Reviewing these areas should help you get clear about what I mean by agentive technology and what lies beyond the scope of my consideration.

It's Not Assistive Technology

Artificial narrow intelligences that help you perform a task are best described as assistants, or assistive technology. We need to think as clearly about assistive tech as we do agentive tech, but we have a solid foundation to design assistive tech. We have been working on those foundations for the last seven decades or so, and recent work with heads-up displays and conversational UI are making headway into best practices for assistants. It's worth noting that the design of agentive systems will often entail designing assistive aspects, but they are not the same thing.

It seems subtle at first, but consider the difference between two ways to get an international airline ticket to a favorite destination. Assistive technology would work to make all your options and the trade-offs between them apparent, helping you avoid spending too much money or winding up with a miserable, five-layover flight, as you make your selection. An agent would vigilantly watch all airline offers for the right ticket and pipe up when it had found one already within your preferences. If it was very confident and you had authorized it, it might even have made the purchase for you.

It's Not Conversational Agents

"Agent" has been used traditionally in services to mean "someone who helps you." Think of a customer service agent. The help they give you is, 99 percent of the time, synchronous. They help you in real time, in person, or on the phone, doing their best to minimize your wait. In my mind, this is much more akin to an *assistant*. But even that's troubling since "assistant" has also been used to mean "that person who helps me at my job" both synchronously—as in "please take dictation"—and agentively—as in "hold all my calls until further notice."

These blurry usages are made even blurrier because human agents and assistants can act in both agentive and assistive ways. But since I have to pick, given the base meanings of the words, I think an assistant should *assist* you with a task, and an agent *takes agency* and does things for you. So "agent" and "agentive" are the right terms for what I'm talking about.

Complicating that rightness is that a recent trend in interaction design is the use of conversational user interfaces, or chatbots. These are distinguished for having users work in a command line interface inside a chat framework, interacting with software that is pretty good at understanding and responding to natural language. Canonical examples feature users purchasing airline tickets (yes, like a travel agent) or movie tickets.

Because these mimic the conversations one might have with a customer service agent, they have been called *conversational agents.*

I think they would be better described as *conversational assistants*, but nobody asked me, and now it's too late. That ship has sailed. So, when I speak of agents, I am not talking about conversational agents. Agentive technology might engage its user through a conversational UI, but they are not the same thing.

It's Not Robots

No. But holy processor do we love them. From *Metropolis'* Maria to BB-8 and even GLaDOS, we just can't stop talking and thinking about them in our narratives.

A main reason I think this is the case is because they're easy to think about. We have lots of mental equipment for dealing with humans, and robots can be thought of as a metal-and-plastic human. So between the *abstraction* that is an agent, and the concrete *thing* that is a robot, it's easy to conflate the two. But we shouldn't.

Another reason is that robots promise—as do agents—"ethics-free" slave labor (please note the irony marks, and see Chapter 12 "Utopia, Dystopia, and Cat Videos" for plenty of ethical questions). In this line of thinking, agents work for us, like slaves, but we don't have to concern ourselves about their subservience or even *subjugation* the same way we must consider a human, because the agents and robots are *programmed* to be of service. There is no suffering sentience there, no longing to be free. For example, if you told your Nest Thermostat to pursue its dreams, it should rightly reply that its dream is to keep you comfortable year round. Programming it for anything else might frustrate the user, and if it is a general artificial intelligence, be cruel to the agent.

Of course, robots will have software running them, which if they are to be useful, will be at times agentive. But while our expectations are that the robot's agent stays in place, coupled as we are to a body, that's not necessarily the case with an agent. For example, my health agent may reside on my phone for the most part, but tap into my bathroom scale when I step on it, parley with the menu when I'm at a restaurant, pop onto the crosstrainer at the gym, and jump to the doctor's augmented reality system when I'm in her office. So while a robot may house agentive technology, and an agent may sometimes occupy a given robot, these two elements are not tightly coupled.

It's Not Service by Software

I actually think this is a very useful way to think about agentive tech: service delivered by smart software. If you have studied service design, then you have a good grounding in the user-centered issues around agentive design. Users often grant agency to services to act on their behalf. For example, I grant the mail service agency to deliver letters on my behalf and agree to receive letters from others. I grant my representative in government agency to legislate on my behalf. I grant the human stock portfolio manager agency to do right by my retirement. I grant the anesthesiologist agency to keep me knocked out while keeping me alive, even though I may never meet her.

But where a service delivers its value through humans working directly with the user or delivering the value "backstage," out of sight, an agent's backstage is its *programming* and the coordination with other agents. In practice, sophisticated agents may entail human processes, but on balance, if it's mostly software, it's an *agent* rather than a *service*. And where a service designer can presume the basic common senses and capabilities of any human in its design, those things need to be handled much differently when we're counting on software to deliver the same thing.

It's Not Automation

If you are a distinguished, long-time student of human-computer interaction, you will note similar themes from the study of automation and what I'm describing. But where automation has as its goal the removal of the human from the system, agentive technology is explicitly in service to a human. An agent might have some automated components, but the intentions of the two fields of study are distinct.

Hey Wait—Isn't Every Technology an Agent?

Hello, philosopher. You've been waiting to ask this question, haven't you? A light switch, you might argue, acts as an agent, monitoring a data stream that is the position of the knife switch. And when that switch changes, it turns the light on or off, accordingly.

Similarly, a key on a keyboard watches its momentary switch and when it is depressed, helpfully sends a signal to a small processor on the keyboard to translate the press to an ASCII code that gets delivered to the software that accumulates these codes to do something with them. And it does it all on your behalf. So are keys agents? Are all state-based machines? Is it turtles all the way down?

Yes, if you want to be philosophical about it, that argument could be made. But I'm not sure how useful it is. A useful definition of agentive technology is less of a discrete and testable aspect of a given technology, and more of a productive way for product managers, designers, users, and citizens to think about this technology. For example, I can design a light switch when I think of it as a product, subject to industrial design decisions. But I can design a *better* light switch when I think of it as a problem that can be solved either *manually* with a switch or *agentively* with a motion detector or a camera with sophisticated image processing behind it. And that's where the real power of the concept comes from. Because as we continue to evolve this skin of technology that increasingly covers both our biology and the world, we don't want it to add to people's burdens. We want to alleviate them and empower people to get done what needs to be done, even if we don't want to do it. And for that, we need agents.

To bring this working definition home, let me end this section by forwarding some practical questions you can ask of a given user task that recurs with some predictability. If the answer to all these is *yes*, then you should probably employ an agentive solution.

- Can the user reasonably delegate tasks off to another? Students learning a language cannot hand that task to an agent and expect to acquire the skill. Similarly, I cannot send an agent to the gym in the hopes of building up muscle. Ethically, I should not accept a paycheck to perform a task that I then secretly hand off to an agent to do it for me.

- Can the trigger for the task be reliably handled by a computer? If, for example, the triggering event is a question of subjective judgment, then a person should handle initiation and most probably execution of the task.

- Does the user have a need for focused attention on some aspect of its performance? If not, why bother the user?

- Can the task be reliably performed with no user input, including preferences and goals? If it can, then why bother the user with it at all?

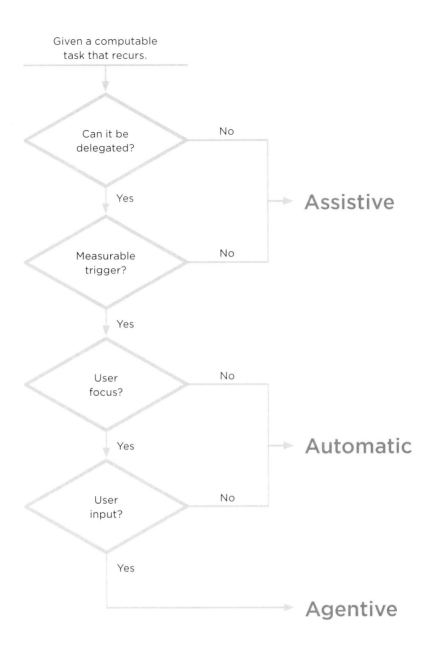

Given a computable
task that recurs.

Can it be
delegated? → No

Yes

Measurable
trigger? → No

→ Assistive

Yes

User
focus? → No

Yes

→ Automatic

User
input? → No

Yes

→ Agentive

Recap: Agents Are Persistent, Background Assistants

Far from being a one-off invention in the form of the thermostat, agentive technologies are appearing all around us, for many long-standing human problems. We can see them if we train ourselves to understand how they're different.

They are

- Software that persists.

- Watching a data stream (or many) for triggers.

- Performing a task for a user according to their goals and preferences.

They are not

- Tech that assists a user with the performance of a task. That's assistive tech.

- Conversational "agents," which are properly thought of as assistants.

- Robots, the software for which is tightly coupled to the hardware. An agent may embody a robot, and a robot may operate as an agent.

- Automation, in which the human is incidental or minimized.

They are different in that

- A valet is the model.

- Design focuses on easy setup and informative touchpoints.

- When it's working, it's most often out of sight.

- Touchpoints require conscious attention and consideration.

- The goals of touchpoints are information, course correction, and helping the agent keep on track.

CHAPTER 3

Agentive Tech Can Change the World

In the first chapter, we walked through the details of one particular example of an agentive technology and deconstructed it bit by bit in the second chapter to better understand what makes this type of tech different. Let's now look at lots of examples to see what makes them really, really cool.

They Move Us from Moments to Interests

The design of tools focuses very much on the moment of use, as it pertains to some task or goal. That means design attention is given to things like the affordances of the interface, mapping of well-designed controls, and meaningful feedback across many layers of interaction. It's the see-think-do loop that is the irreducible atom of interaction design.

Much of the benefit of using an agent is that it can persistently look for things the user didn't even know specifically existed, like a nice shirt, a mention on the web, or a new recording by a favorite artist. For these reasons, setting up a search with an agent isn't about setting up filters for what's out there now, but more about what could be out there in the future. It's about telling the agent what interests you.

Google Alerts: General Interest

To start with an understatement, most people are aware of Google as a search engine. Type "agentive" into its search bar and see the results of web pages, news items, and images on the web now. (And if you're wondering, at the time of publication, this results in very little, since I'm at the beginning of my quest to rescue the word from obscurity.) But at www.google.com/alerts, you can set up a persistent search where an agent will email you when anything new matching your search terms is published in its news, blog, and web feeds.

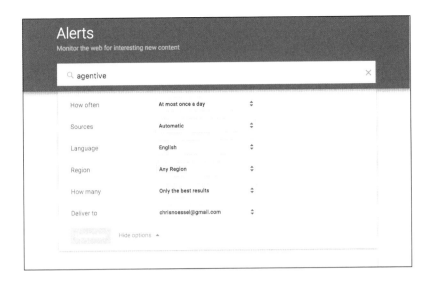

Using this, you can set up alerts for almost anything of interest. If it can be found with a basic text Google search, it can be turned into an Alert.

Google even has examples of well-formed Alert searches of possible interest. That gives users an easy opt-in for likely interests, but also shows them examples from which they can learn to construct new ones (even if most are blatant marketing).

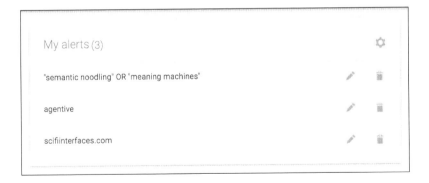

Using these tools, you tell the agent what you're interested in, and it helps you stay on top of it. But interests aren't just limited to mentions. It can be when favorite recording artists publish new works.

iTunes Follow: Music Interests

If you use iTunes, there are two aspects that are agentive: the smart playlist and the Follow feature.

Regular playlists are dumb collections of songs. (No, no, your taste in music is impeccable. I mean the software logic of this type of list is not *smart*.) You can edit the list manually, but the list will stay like that until you change it again.

Smart playlists, on the other hand, let you select the features of the song you want in the playlist. Then the playlist acts as an agent when your music collection changes to see if any of the new songs fit the playlist's definition. If so, Live Updating automatically adds it in.

As long as I've got songs tagged with beats-per-minute, this definition will create a cardio playlist of songs that will keep me charged and that I like. A small thing, for sure, but it lets me describe my interests and lets the agentive tech do the rest.

The Follow feature is another aspect. Visit an artist page in iTunes, and you'll find a Follow control. (At the time of writing you have to be subscribed to Apple Music, and then it appears in a drop-down list under a blue button at the right-hand side of the page.) Click it, and hey, now you're following that artist.

iTunes doesn't bother to explain what the actual consequences are for hitting this toggle, but nonetheless, a quick Google search reveals that they will send you an email when any of the recording artists you're following has a new release available.

A better agent might recognize that I have an interest in more than just music releases. I might be interested in knowing when that artist is on tour near me (or near where I might be traveling), or has an interview, or releases a new video online, but that task might befit the Google Alerts agent better. However, interests aren't just limited to digital goods, either. They can be physical.

eBay Followed Searches: Interests in Stuff

Most folks know of eBay as a great place to go and find something to purchase at a good price, but it also has an agentive feature called *Followed Searches*. Launched back in 1999 as the *Personal Shopper*, this feature lets users take any search and keep it going. Even if I don't find one right now in a style, size, and price I want, I can ask the site to keep an eye on all new items that go on sale there for me, and let me know when any match.

eBay has search tools for that moment I hope to find something for now, and agentive tools to help me keep track of things I'm interested in.

What's interesting for the kind of search embodied in these three agentive examples is that creating too specific of a search term can work against you. Following a search for "green Ted Baker shirts selling for $53 in San Francisco" might find you exactly the shirt you're looking for right now, but it would not provide a fruitful persistent search in the future. Users need to be able to set up more abstract searches, and agents may need to help them do it.

These kinds of persistent searches move you from having to go out and find stuff of interest yourself to letting stuff of interest find you—for example, to subscribe to your favorite artists (or authors) or to notify you when cool things are mentioned online. The dark side of this might be opt-out advertising, but in the best cases, these agents turn the tables so that your interests find you. How will marketing and advertising change when this becomes the norm?

They'll Do the Work You're Not Good At

Autopilots are handy because getting from point A to far-away point B can be monotonous in the middle, and people aren't reliable at those kinds of attention-endurance tasks. Fortunately, for the past century, people have been developing systems to help with that part of the journey in boats, planes, and increasingly, cars.

Autohelm Steers the Boat

Boat captains navigating easy seas simply need to keep the boat pointed in the same direction. Early mechanical systems worked by using a wind vane to keep the boat at the same angle against the wind. Today these systems are known by a couple of names, with *marine autopilots* being the most common and *autohelm* being a genericized trademark of Raymarine's product line (which nicely distinguishes it from aviation autopilots). In their simplest mode, the captain presses the AUTO button, demonstrates the angle at which it must be held, and then lets go to attend to other things around the boat, like perhaps a nice hot buttered rum or the next track of yacht rock.

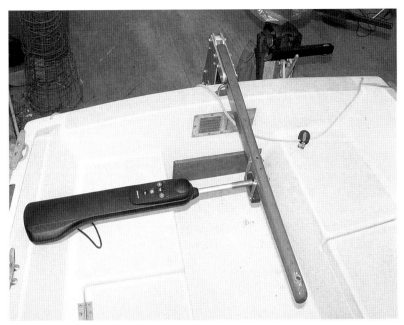

More expensive configurations pair with GPS, sonar, and course-plotting devices to make the autohelm aware of the heading, obstacles above and below the water, location (and corresponding maritime law), and planned course. Touching the tiller or ship's wheel can be the exception and not the rule.

Understanding this function of the autohelm, it's easy to see how a captain on a short pleasure ride might get distracted by other things on the boat and need to recover quickly when she finds herself off course or hears the drone of an alarm from the autohelm, or finds her vessel in all sorts of possible trouble. Since the device is an add-on to the normal mechanics of a ship, the pilot can use normal means to assess the problem, quickly disengage the device to take manual control if necessary, or troubleshoot the electronics if the problem is the technology itself.

Autoflight Pilots the Plane

Airplane pilots have to manage more complex variables with less margin for error than their maritime counterparts, but long trips can still be fatiguing. The earliest mechanical autopilots worked like the simple autohelm, but with rudder control being augmented by an attitude sensor adjusting the plane's horizontal tail flaps, or elevators. Nowadays, autopilots are required for most long-range passenger planes over a certain size, and they consist of many subsystem controls for altitude, speed, throttle, heading, and course. While airplane pilots are always busy and can't just zone out, they do rely on the autoflight systems to manage some of the tedious aspects of flying and to warn them when there is a problem.

WIKIMEDIA COMMONS HTTPS://EN.WIKIPEDIA.ORG/WIKI/AUTOPILOT

Don Norman has studied the interaction of pilots with autopilot. Norman estimates that a pilot flying at 25,000 feet up has about five minutes to figure out that there's something wrong, then decide what's going wrong, and finally to recover in order to save the plane and the people aboard.

Autodrive Drives the Car

Even though driverless cars aren't yet common on roads, we're already dealing with autodrive. (Aside: Dear future, forgive us. We're still in that transitional phase where we have to call them "driverless," to distinguish them from the "manually driven" variety, but you'll know them simply as "cars.") Manufacturers like Tesla, Volvo, and Mercedes-Benz car models have the driver facing forward, ready to take over. Google's driverless cars are eventually meant to be wholly agentive, so there won't be any need for passengers to suddenly take control. But in the near term, while the technology is being introduced to roads, riders and even legislators[1] are most comfortable with a driver sitting at the helm of the driverless car, ready to take over should the agent fail.

COURTESY OF GOOGLE

But if a, uhhh, "driver" is just sitting there not driving, can they really stay, just sitting there, keeping their attention on their non-task constantly? Ten seconds is all it takes for a user's attention to drift while using slow software, and I'm pretty sure a car trip won't be worth taking if it's under ten seconds long. Perhaps the car will have to introduce some means of keeping the driver actively engaged in the driving, such as a game that drivers play by trying to match the software's driving. But if not, then the sitrep-and-takeover will present major problems to the driver who's just about to win a difficult, timed game on their phone and has to drop that to wonder what that alarm is all about.

They'll Do the Things We're Unwilling to Do

ShotSpotter is a civic agent that constantly listens to a large number of microphones that are sprinkled across a neighborhood. When it hears gunshots, it compares the timestamp on each microphone to triangulate the location of the shots to within a meter's accuracy. Within seconds of the gunfire, officers can be on their way to investigate.

---

1 http://spectrum.ieee.org/cars-that-think/transportation/self-driving/
  google-reported-to-be-setting-up-standalone-robocar-ridesharing-service

Agents do things for you while your attention is elsewhere. That's an awesome way to maximize your time, but it can pose a major challenge If you and others are relying on the agent to do its job, and it runs into a problem big enough that it needs someone to take over quickly to avert a crisis. How does a person get up to speed quickly on the state of things? What is the troublesome thing and what's troublesome about it? What does the user need to do to remedy things, what are the options and recommended actions, and how is the handoff between agent-control and manual-control handled? Will it be active, like manually removing the autotiller device from the tiller, or more passive, like simply grabbing the wheel and canceling cruise control? How fast will this handoff have to happen, and how can we make it efficient?

These are new questions for interaction design that will be fun and important to answer. But with more and more travel being handled by agents, it promises not just to become safer and more efficient overall, but also to give riders more time to do things that interest them, only occasionally needing to manage the vehicle. These issues are important enough to warrant two chapters in this book. See Chapter 8, "Handling Exceptions," and Chapter 9, "Handoff and Takeback," in Part II.

When I spoke with a representative from ShotSpotter, she explained that the service is helpful for more reasons than just decreased police response time. It also helps ensure that the "shots fired" signal reaches the police *at all*. One factor is the bystander effect, in which people presume that surely someone else has reported it already. This might affect people living anywhere. But citizens living in high-crime areas, she explained, can often fear being labeled a snitch and suffering consequences for reporting crimes. ShotSpotter takes this responsibility that no one wants unto itself.

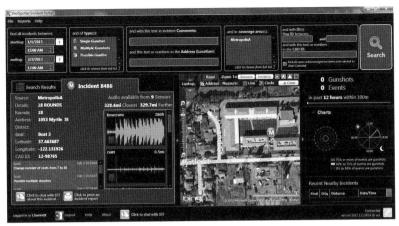

They'll Do the Embarrassing Things

Going on first dates can be harrowing. Who knows if that person is genuinely charming, or a well-practiced sociopath? You should have a backup, someone who will check up on you. But then again, you don't want to burden friends with remote chaperone duties for every single date you go on. Enter the safety agent that is kitestring.io. You tell Kitestring when to check up on you, information about the date you're going on, and an emergency contact. When time is up, Kitestring sends you a text to make sure you're OK. If you don't answer, or reply with your *fake* safe word, it forwards the information about the date to the emergency contact, presumably so they can take immediate action to find you and ensure your safety. If you answer with the *real* safe word, Kitestring erases the information about the date and stops checking up on you. It's not a replacement for being careful, but an additional tool in your arsenal.

They Will Allow Play . . .

In some domains, users are happy to let the agent run, and only think about it when there's a problem. Managing a long-term invest-ment portfolio is one where you specifically don't want to look at it every day. But in other domains, you'll need to recognize that users will still want to play.

Here I'm thinking of iOS AutoCorrect. (It's closer to assistive tech, but is still an instructive example for our purposes here.) In this low-level typing function, if users mistype a word (or correctly type an unusual word that is not in its dictionary), the operating system will offer to replace the word with its best guess of the intended word. Spell-checks have been around almost since the beginning of computers, but AutoCorrect has two differences. First, the interaction design is such that most of the time, people don't realize their words have been autocorrected until after they've sent text messages or made status updates. Second, being on a mobile OS with an on-screen keyboard means there are plenty of mistakes to be corrected.

Most of the time, AutoCorrect works pretty seamlessly, changing people's mitsakes to mistakes before they realize they've happened. Some of the time the corrections are nonsensical. And a few times they can be genuinely funny.

But if you are a playful user of language, AutoCorrect is much more of a damned nuisance than a help. There's a whole philosophical tangent I'll avoid about why being a playful user of language is important at any age, but even if you're personally prudish with your words, note that it's a fact of teenage life and part of the currency of subcultures. It's a way to create and celebrate a shared identity. Consider the recent popularity of "turnt," "bae," "yas," and "nudnik." OK, that last one is from the 1920s, but a flapper with an iPhone, can you *imagine*? Since both declining the autocorrections and adding to its dictionary slow your text entry down significantly, it's much easier to just turn the feature completely off. Better would be an agent that gauges your degree of playfulness, or updates itself with language trends of your peers, and backs off accordingly.

(Note that we are on the *second* edition of *Damn You Auto Correct* compilations from the blog of the same name, so it's kind of a *thing*.)

... and They Will Encourage Discovery Through *Drift*

IBM has been working on its deep learning engine Watson since 2005.[2] Although its first public implementation was to compete against humans on the game show *Jeopardy!*, since winning that show in 2011, the project has evolved in some other directions. Chef Watson is one spinoff that came online in 2015. At first, it seems like any other recipe database: a search form lets you input ingredients to find recipes.

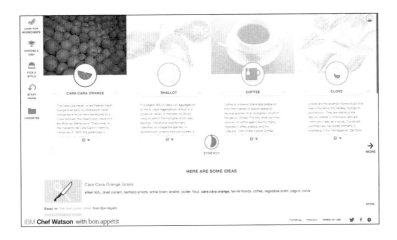

But there are several fantastic things about Chef Watson that make it different. For one, it automatically searches for other ingredients based on "synergy" with your starting ingredient, for example, the presence of similarly flavored chemical compounds. Next, it finds existing recipes for the set of ingredients, and it "drifts" them. By drifting (my term), I mean taking a known recipe and finding replacements for ingredients. For instance, with a *little* drift, a lemon tart might become a lime tart, and with a *lot* of drift it might become a mangosteen tart. Or perhaps a Yuzu Kouign-amann. Seriously, this software will surprise you. In the pictured example, Chef Watson has taken the recipe for Tea and Lemon Gravy from *Bon Appétit* and drifted it so that the Cara Cara orange replaces the lemon.

---

2 https://en.wikipedia.org/wiki/Watson_(computer)

Additionally, it checks its database to ensure that the starting point it gives you is unique. As far as it knows, that recipe has never been tried before in recorded history. That's a pretty amazing thought. Sure, you're going to run into some culinary dead ends, but think about what deliciousness you're going to discover.

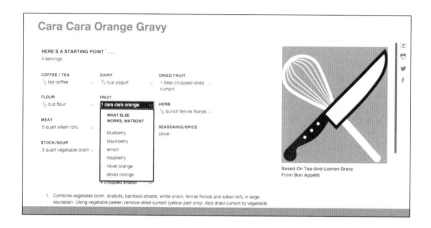

But hang on, it even goes one better, because Chef Watson knows, *Hey, I'm just a computer semi-randomly modifying recipes, not a human with taste buds* (and limited by access to ingredients—think you'll find a yuzu at your local bodega?). So it lets users drift recipes manually, too. In the above picture, I've clicked on one cara cara orange to see that I can pick any of the fruits in the list to suit my tastes or drift it further.

In true agentive form, Chef Watson even lets me store my food preferences (ovo-lacto vegetarian, distaste for mushroom and sea flavors) and will send me recipes occasionally based on the general calendar. In the future, I fully expect to give it permission to look at my personal calendar and receive suggestions when I am booked for a potluck.

Between play and drift, your agents won't ask you to adhere to rigid rules, but rather to channel and encourage creativity and discovery, all while making it easy to make smart choices.

They Help Achieve Goals with Minimal Effort

Tasks by definition are small things, bound by time or the simplicity of their undertaking, but performed by people in the service of some larger goal. For instance, a person can take photos (task) to preserve the happy vacation memories for a group of friends (goal). Another person can take photos (the same task) to capture the elusive beauty of natural forms (goal). Most of design focuses on designing for the task, and that can produce perfectly functional things, but design that focuses on users' goals are much more *loved* because they help us do so much more. They fit into our lives and identities. You can even say that an agent is the ultimate expression of goal-focused design thinking, because it gets users to their goals with the least effort possible.

That simple design principle explains why agentive tech that is focused on the goal will win out over agents that focus on the task. Take, for example, cameras. Point-and-shoot cameras have existed for a long time now, but these tools eliminate the work of managing all the complex and interrelated settings involved in taking a picture—but you're still taking a picture. Contrast that with the life blog cameras like the Narrative Clip. It's a small square device with a clip on the back and a small lens on the front. As long as the lens sees light, it takes a picture every 30 seconds. Clip it on your shirt, and by the end of the day, you'll have around 2,000 pictures. That would be an overwhelming number to sort and sift through, except the Narrative uploads all the images it took to a server, where smart algorithms first divide them into segments of the day, pick the best ones from each segment, and share those good few with you via an app. The app lets you second-guess its selections and annotate or share them on social media. So as you can see, it is *kind-of* a camera. But it's also not. It's an *agentive* camera that focuses on your living life and having great photos, rather than taking photos.

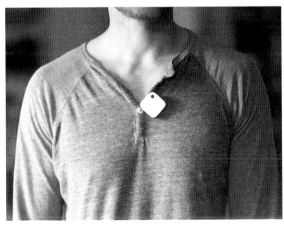

COURTESY OF NARRATIVE

Similarly, the Roomba is a vacuum unlike the ones that came before it. The goal of the design of prior vacuum cleaners was to make it light, powerful, and ergonomic, i.e., to make it easy for a user to clean their floors. But the Roomba rethinks the problem. It's an agentive vacuum that sits in its charging cradle until scheduled cleaning times. Then it roams around vacuuming until it gets close to running out of battery, when it returns to the cradle. In typical use, users only have to empty its dustbin occasionally.

COURTESY OF iROBOT

Both the Narrative Clip and the Roomba turn the tables on their predecessors by focusing on meeting the goal with an agentive technology, rather than being a good tool for users to complete tasks.

The Scenario Is—a Lifetime

Most technologies focus on the moment of use. Even the tools you use to embody users, i.e., personas, are typically tied to an age, a small moment in time. But since agents handle things for their users over the long haul, agentive technology encourages you to think about the scenarios that make up a whole life.

Betterment is a roboinvestor that helps users keep investment portfolios balanced to specific risk targets. It lets investors specify long-term goals—from drawing a particular income in retirement to making a down payment on a home. Since these are long-term goals—playing out across decades—they have to take into account the change in persona goals from when they are young, bright-eyed, and bushy tailed, to when they're about to hit retirement and be cautious about losing what they've gained, all the way through retirement, drawing down on their savings and enjoying their golden years.

Technology is accelerating. It's hard to know exactly what the world or technology will look like in five or ten years, so the far-horizon scenarios can be more aspirational and even vague. But agentive tech encourages you to take this long-term view and at least think about how it might be, knowing what you know now.

There May Be an Arms Race of Competing Agents

In this book, I speak mostly about agents acting on behalf of users with benign intentions, but let's not be Pollyanna about it. Bad actors are out there, causing mayhem and trying to separate you from your hard-earned money. Fortunately, you're already quite familiar with one agent who does its work almost entirely in the background, saving you from Nigerian Princes and the tedium of unwanted sales messages—that's the humble spam filter.

You may not think about it as an agent, but that's what it is. Persistently on, it looks at every incoming message for telltale signs of *spamness*, sent from any accounts that have been confirmed as spammers, as well as any senders that you've personally blocked or personally blessed. And these it silently sweeps into a folder that you're free to check anytime, but from which it clears out old messages on a regular basis.

Sadly, for every advancement in spam filters, spammers will seek some new way around them. They're always there. They're like raptors, testing the fences, trying new strategies. But spam and its related scourge, computer viruses, are enough of a hassle that your immune system filters will keep evolving with them.

It's Going to Be Big Enough to Affect Our Infrastructure

I spoke about self-driving cars earlier in this chapter. And in addition to the question of what you're doing while you're in them—monitoring and ready to take the wheel at a moment's notice or catching up on the latest holo-toons—what's even more interesting are the conversations about what these cars will be doing when you're *not* in them.

COURTESY OF MERCEDES-BENZ

They could just park themselves in your garage, driveway, or find a spot on a nearby street. But given agentive cars, why would they do that? They could attend to the small amount of taxi demand for cars at night, earning some money for their owner. They could drive themselves for maintenance or cleaning. They could be rented as a nighttime delivery vehicle, or as a remote-controlled, mobile sensor network for urban planners, scientists, and first responders.

If they're not being used in any of these ways, they still don't need to park right near you as long as they can get back to you by the time you need them again. Could they find otherwise unused spaces, allowing homeowners to reclaim driveways for human purposes? Or could they park on a designated lane on a nearby freeway until they're needed?

Whatever the answer is, we're going to need to rethink the urban landscape for new efficiencies when agentive things can move themselves out of the way. This will allow us to take some of the massive percentage of urban land use dedicated to parking (in L.A. it's estimated to be as high as 14% of the total) and reclaim it for people.

Places and Objects Will Need Them

Places and objects have needs. Since the dawn of time, we as their users have needed to routinely keep tabs on them to see if they need maintenance of some sort. Do the kitchen knives need sharpening? Does the office have enough Post-it Notes? Do we need to air out the garage from fumes? But if these places and objects are imbued with agentive technology, we can offload that monitoring onto the things themselves. The knife block can watch the knives for when they need sharpening. The supplies closet can send emails when the paper is low. The garage can watch the air for problems. The responsiveness of objects is captured in conversations around the Internet of Things, but it's instructive to think of the *Thing* in IoT as a place that agents inhabit.

A striking example is represented by the services offered by GOBI Library Solutions to academic libraries. Most people don't think about it, but managing the collections of tens of thousands of books is a major undertaking. Librarians have to keep an eye on the demand of esoteric subjects they themselves may know nothing about, and they must continually adjust the collection to match need. GOBI's demand-driven acquisitions is an agent that keeps tabs on the borrowing database for the library; both when patrons borrow books from the collection and when the library must borrow from another library to meet demand. It then routinely performs an analysis to determine how the collection needs to adjust, and can send orders for those books with the budget approval of the collections manager. It is an agent that works with the librarians to keep the knowledge base as relevant as possible to the changing needs of its users.

People have similar needs managing places and objects. How about a plant that lets you know when it's thirsty? Or a civic agent to let you know what museum exhibits touring through town would interest you?

They Will Help Us Overcome Some Human Foibles

For all our awesomeness, humans have some built-in foibles that are really hard for us to overcome. (Check out the full *List of Cognitive Biases* on Wikipedia if you want a deep dive.[3]) Any time we humans perform a task, we carry those biases with us. They can interfere with our effectiveness. Those foibles may be minor for the individual, but can add up to serious problems when aggregated up to the level of cities, nation-states, or a planet. Traffic is an example most everyone is familiar with. It's stressful and wasteful to sit in traffic, and moving feels better, so people try to find shortcuts that ultimately cost them more time, use more gasoline, and can cause further traffic snarls for everyone else.

But that problem can be addressed when wayfinding is handled by an agentive app. The community-based traffic and navigation app, Waze, has a number of nice agentive features, but for purposes of this point, let's look at traffic distribution. It constantly re-evaluates an individual's routing to determine if taking an alternate route—including side streets and shortcuts—would actually buy that driver more time. If it doesn't, it keeps to the current plan. But if a reroute would mean more time, it alerts the driver that a faster route is available and lets them opt-in. This recommendation is based on actual, real-time data rather than our simple lizard-brain emotions, and ensures that traffic as a whole is being routed across the map in an actually efficient way.

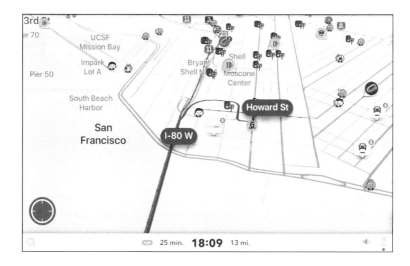

---

3 https://en.wikipedia.org/wiki/List_of_cognitive_biases

In addition to being freer from our cognitive biases (simply by dint of being algorithms), we can go one step further by adding virtues in. Imagine the agentive car that coordinates with other cars to distribute its rider's journeys across time as well as routes. Could agents be programmed to avoid other *tragedies of the commons*?

Using Them, People Will Program the World

Conversations about Pervasive or Ubiquitous Computing have been around since the late 1980s, but we're now living it. It's difficult to walk in public out of the view of a camera. We're carrying and wearing more computing power than it took early astronauts to get to the moon. The technological skin of the planet is evolving and growing all the time, and its disparate parts can be connected by one of the most abstract agentive technologies that is out there.

The *If This Then That* service (ifttt.com) allows you to create persistent formulas, called *recipes*, which are exactly what the name implies. If the specified triggers are met (*the this*), then the service carries out the actions (*the that*). And that's it. Each recipe acts like a little agent, watching and measuring the pertinent data stream until it gets to perform its action, and then it settles back down again, eyes firmly on the stream.

Triggers can be made more aware by connecting different data streams: social media, car computers, calendars, email, and phone sensors. Actions can be made more powerful by authorizing the service to add to your social media stream, to text or email you, to control your home automation system, or to create documents that capture important data.

Some of these are pretty basic. One recipe looks for rain in the forecast and sends you a text each morning if you need to take along an umbrella. Another keeps your profile pictures in sync across social media services. If you have a connected car, one can send you an email with a map every time you park in the city.[4, 5, 6]

Authors can make their recipes public, and there are many vast collections of recipes—for work, home, music, health, and even outer space. IFTTT is a huge collection of tiny agents that are all making the world a more connected space. Ultimately, I believe that large brands will offer some of these as features of their products and services, but it's really nice to have an independent service that gives people a platform to play.

Our Species' Future May Well Depend on Them

I know, that header sounds overblown. But hear me out. You know how in 600 million years, the increasing brightness of the sun will interrupt the carbonate-silicate geophysical cycle, ultimately interrupting plate tectonics, halting volcanic activity, and stopping C3 photosynthesis? Six hundred million years sounds like a long time until you recall that life is estimated to have begun on this planet around three billion years ago. If we've only got one billion left, life is *way* over half done. Which means that—presuming we make it that far—we'll have to migrate from this planet to another. Ultimately, space travel is the only way our species will survive, and space exploration is a critical part of that.

---

4 https://ifttt.com/recipes/634-add-a-calendar-event-for-bringing-an-umbrella-in-the-morning-when-the-forecast-calls-for-rain

5 https://ifttt.com/recipes/8981-keep-your-profile-pictures-in-sync

6 https://ifttt.com/recipes/346212-receive-an-email-with-a-map-to-where-you-just-parked

ILLUSTRATION OF MARS CURIOSITY ROVER, COURTESY OF NASA

Fortunately, that's already underway, and it's being done smartly with robots that don't have our messy, frail, and expensive biological requirements. But space exploration quickly runs into a problem of communication time. Even light speed communications have limits. Sending a message to just Mars involves a 4- to 24-minute delay (depending on our positions in orbit), and even if replies are instantaneous, adds up to an 8- to 48-minute delay between back-and-forth responses. That's not too bad. NASA's Mars rover won't get into too much trouble in that time.

But the farther out it travels, the longer that delay is. Jupiter is between one and two hours. Pluto is roughly once per day. The farther out we travel, the more time there will be between our communications with exploration robots, and the more we will need the robots to handle things on their own. What should it do if it encounters an immediate problem or opportunity, flying through the blackness of space, or rambling over the cold stones of a distant planet? We need to equip these representatives with the right sensors, actuators, rules, and exceptions to learn what it can learn, send the information back to us, and still keep exploring. Fortunately, this isn't some gaping hole in space exploration strategy. It's a known problem, and NASA is already on the case, with its Remote Agent Architecture,[7] or RAA.

---

7 https://ti.arc.nasa.gov/m/pub-archive/77h/0077%20(Dorais).pdf

Recap: Yes, the World

We're going to stop searching for things and instead register our interests. Agents will keep us up-to-date on cool stuff. We're going to give agents our most tedious tasks, and only need to get involved when they run into some truly unusual situations. They'll help us manage the transition to being in control. They'll help us with our goals across our entire lives, but minimize the effort it takes to get there. They'll introduce new efficiencies on a macro level, letting us reclaim those resources for other things. If we program them well, they'll help us act more rationally as a species, freeing up some of the biases that have plagued us. We will use them to connect the disparate digital services with which we manage our limited time on this Earth, even to the extent of helping us get off of it when the time comes.

And you thought I was exaggerating with the chapter title.

There are more examples of agentive technology out there, but the ones included in this chapter should work to give us a lot to draw from for the rest of the book, and illustrate that once you are able to distinguish the power and promise of agentive technology, it's hard *not* to see how it is going to change the world, even if we never make it to an artificial general intelligence like HAL.

CHAPTER 4

Six Takeaways from the History of Agentive Thinking

When I describe agentive tech as "new," it's in air quotes, as a nod to the fact that in some form or another, these ideas have a very long history. You just have to know where to look to find them. Within the past 100 years, engineering was mad for *automation* in the 1950s and 1960s. A group thought through control systems as *cybernetics* in the 1960s to the 1980s. Academia was interested in agents throughout the 1990s. (Nowadays they're more likely to be writing about cooperation between agents and computer-supported cooperative work, or CSCW.) In the 2000s, businesses like IBM have adapted the ideas into their practice with things like "cognitive computing" or Intel's interest in "proactive computing."

Product management and interaction design are only now coming around to it, but we should acknowledge the great thinking that has come before. This chapter gives an overview of the key takeaways that I've found from studying the writings, papers, and lecturers in the field in the course of writing this book. I'm just one nerd, though, and haven't read everything out there. I encourage you to follow up on any of the authors, publications, or topics that pique your interest.

To begin, let's go back to a time when one woman's face "launch'd a thousand ships" to war, and even the gods themselves got caught up in the action.

> ...Meanwhile Thetis came to the house of Vulcan, imperishable, star-bespangled, fairest of the abodes in heaven, a house of bronze wrought by the lame god's own hands. She found him busy with his bellows, sweating and hard at work, for he was making twenty tripods that were to stand by the wall of his house, and he set wheels of gold under them all that they might go of their own selves to the assemblies of the gods, and come back again, marvels indeed to see. They were finished all but the ears of cunning workmanship which yet remained to be fixed to them: these he was now fixing, and he was hammering at the rivets.
>
> [Hearing Thetis has arrived from his wife Charis, Vulcan says,] "...If then Thetis has come to my house I must make her due requital for having saved me; entertain her, therefore, with all hospitality, while I put by my bellows and all my tools."
>
> On this the mighty monster hobbled off from his anvil, his thin legs plying lustily under him. He set the bellows away from the fire, and gathered his tools into a silver chest. Then he took a

sponge and washed his face and hands, his shaggy chest and
brawny neck; he donned his shirt, grasped his strong staff, and
limped towards the door. There were golden handmaids that also
worked for him, and were like real young women, with sense and
reason, voice also and strength, and all the learning of the im-
mortals; these busied themselves as the king bade them, while he
drew near to Thetis, seated her upon a goodly seat, and took her
hand into his own

Homer, *The Iliad*, Book XXVIII
Translated by Samuel Butler

In these passages, we can read Homer's agentive imaginings from
2,750 years ago, of a few of Hephaestus' legendary menagerie of
machines. Tripods were revered objects in ancient Greece, status
objects which often marked ceremonial and holy places. That he
should have 20 of them is itself meant to impress. Then on top of that,
they "go of their own selves" to locations that needed to be marked
as ceremonial and holy. They were the self-driving cars of Olympus.
Or maybe the self-driving decor. Anytime, anywhere stateliness.
I'll also note that his golden handmaidens acted as robot assistants,
equipped with full artificial intelligence and celestial Wikipedias in
their heads. Narrow and general artificial intelligence work side-by-
side in Vulcan's world.

I cite Homer not just because it helps justify my undergraduate
Honors degree, but also to illustrate how long we've been fascinated
with the notion of mechanical agencies that could do our bidding.

It's as Old as Myth

Homer wasn't the only ancient to imagine biddable, non-human
agencies. Jewish mythology tells tales of the golem, a protohuman
made of clay. These figures were able to obey instructions, but had
no sentience. In some delightful wordplay, they had the Hebrew
word "מת" or "dead" inscribed on their forehead. You could activate
them by adding an aleph to this inscription, which changed the word
to "אמת" or "truth." You could deactivate them again by removing
the aleph and returning it to "dead" and death: a fun, tangible user
interface. Some tellings said the golem would obey whatever was
written on a small piece of paper that was placed in its mouth, an
early notion of programming. The golem was an agent because it
would tirelessly do what it was told until it was commanded to stop.

Six Takeaways from the History of Agentive Thinking   55

In the ancient Arabic world, tales are told of the inhuman genies, or djinn, which are sometimes bound to fulfill human wishes. The most popular is the tale of Aladdin from *One Thousand and One Nights*. The djinn that Aladdin meets are agents in that they first monitor their prisons for summoning, i.e., the rub of a ring or a lamp. After they have been summoned, they listen to their masters' wishes (which often must be formatted correctly to begin with "I wish...") and then, of course, grant the wish as stated. Many wish-granting agents or magical objects from folklore like The Monkey's Paw are strict or malicious interpreters, who twist the letter of the wish against the spirit of it, to thwart the wisher. So these stories are also interesting to us as warnings about the need to be precise with instructions, which is an issue with any programming, but even more so with agents, that will enact their instructions away from the supervision of their users.

More recent examples include Goethe's poem *The Sorcerer's Apprentice* (more familiar perhaps to readers by the animated mouse version of the same story), who enchants a broom to do one of his chores for him—i.e., to fetch water by pail. He forgets the magic word by which he can end the enchantment, and before long the house is flooded. Had this broom golem been programmed with a simple aleph switch, that might be the end of it. But the desperate apprentice chops the broom in two with an axe, and owing to the squirrely nature of narrative magic, it then becomes two brooms carrying out the same instruction, twice as fast. At last, the *Deus ex Sorcerer* returns to undo the spell and command the broom to obey only the master.

Our sci-fi concepts of robots are bound in agentive concepts. The maschinenmensch (machine-human) "Maria" from Fritz Lang's *Metropolis* was an early example. She was given the likeness of her human counterpart and tasked to foment insurrection in the Upper City, which she did with flapper precision while her evil master Rotwang carried on with other misdeeds. Even our term "robot" comes from the Czech word for "worker," coined in Karel Čapek's 1921 play *R.U.R.*, which in English stood for *Rossum's Universal Robots*. The machines in this script are sentient but built to be an ethics-free slave labor class, to work for the humans who were enjoying lives of leisure. In this story, at least, the robots rebel and destroy humanity.

Stories are one way that we think about things. We process believable cause and effect. We study the givens and the outcomes. We give ourselves memorable dire warnings and reminders of what's important. But myth and folklore, as analogs for the problem, can only take us so far.

Yes, Virginia, Computers Can Take Initiative

Questions of agency were entwined with the very origins of modern computing. In 1842, Lady Lovelace rejected the notion of agency when she published her memoir of Charles Babbage's Analytical Engine. There she argued that "The Analytical Engine has no pretensions to *originate* anything. It can do *whatever we know how to order it* to perform" (her italics). I submit that this made a lot of people at the time quite comfortable that this genie could be kept in its lamp. But nearly 100 years later in 1949, eminent mathematician and physicist Douglas Hartree added to her comment to note that:

> This does not imply that it may not be possible to construct electronic equipment which will 'think for itself,' or in which, in biological terms, one could set up a conditioned reflex, which would serve as a basis for 'learning.' Whether this is possible in principle or not is a stimulating and exciting question, suggested by some of these recent developments. But it did not seem that the machines constructed or projected at the time had this property.

Hartree's "conditioned reflex" sounds a lot like the triggers that agentive technology is concerned with. Hartree in turn influenced father-of-modern-computing Alan Turing in his writing of the (prepare for an understatement) seminal paper "Computing Machinery and Intelligence" in which he asserted the key components of a state-based machine. This, if it needs saying, is the basis of the thing on which I'm writing this book and on which you are more and more likely to be reading it, and which is the foundation of the technology I'm writing about. So, you know, *seminal*.

Now I'm pleased to note that the question of whether a computer can take initiative is well behind us. It may be that they can only take the initiative that we equip them to, but that's enough. They can take initiative, and increasingly in more sophisticated senses of the word. Agentive technologies are predicated on this.

Automation Doesn't Work Like You Think

In 1951, just one year after Turing published "Computing Machinery and Intelligence," psychologist and efficiency researcher Paul Fitts published his paper "Human Engineering for an Effective Air-Navigation and Traffic-Control System," which is most famous for its so-called "HABA-MABA" lists early in the paper. These lists distinguished what Humans Are Better At (HABA) and what Machines Are Better At (MABA).

HUMANS ARE BETTER AT:

with
respect
Mr.
Fitts

MACHINES ARE BETTER AT:

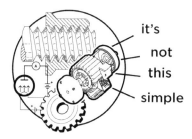

it's
not
this
simple

Humans Are Better At

- Humans can easily access from amongst their years of collected memories the ones that are relevant to a given situation or problem.

- Humans can detect quite slight audio-visual signals.

- Humans can perceive emergent patterns in light and sound.

- Humans can improvise performance and use flexible procedures in the pursuit of a solution.

- Humans are good at inductive reasoning. This allows us to read two givens, such as "All men are mortal" and "Socrates was a man" to infer that "Socrates is mortal."

- Passing judgment on the value or rightness of a thing.

Machines Are Better At

- Machines have perfect short-term memory. Additionally, it is perfectly erasable such that it can avoid the psychological biases of primacy, recency, and hyperbolic discounting.

- Machines can perform tasks and respond to programmed stimuli with great speed.

- Machines can manipulate great forces with speed and precision.

- Machines can maintain consistency across repetitive tasks. They do not suffer boredom.

- Machines are good at deductive reasoning. This is the Sherlock Holmes type of reasoning, which depends on eliminating untrue hypotheses and ranking true hypotheses to determine the remaining set.

- Machines are good at managing simultaneous complex operations.

These lists were quite influential to a generation of thinkers, as well as initial designs of automated systems. The thinking went that if machines are better at those things, then give them those things, and let the humans handle the rest. The implicit frame of this "function allocation" was that a computer was just another sort of worker. But it turns out that's not what happened.

In 1983, Lisanne Bainbridge published the paper "Ironies of Automation" where she took those presumptions to task. Studying autopilots specifically, but speaking about automation generally, she explained what the intervening three decades of efforts toward automation had learned. When you take people away from regular practice at working as part of a system, they become worse at preventing, troubleshooting, and remedying problems in that system. We'll talk more about what this implies for design in Part II, "Doing," but for now let's just acknowledge that counterintuitive fact.

So while Fitts' HABA-MABA lists seem reasonable on the surface, it turns out that they are significantly misleading as to the nature of the problem of coordinating with computer or robotic workers. It's like trying to understand economics by listing which units of money should be paper and which should be coins.

In 2002, the IEEE published the Hoffman–Woods "Anti-Fitts List" in an article poetically called "A Rose by Any Other Name...Would Probably Be Given An Acronym." These new lists tried to unseat the pernicious Fitts list by succinctly describing a different frame.

Machines are constrained in that:

- Sensitivity to context is low and is ontology-limited.
- Sensitivity to change is low and recognition of anomaly is ontology-limited.
- Adaptability to change is low and is ontology-limited.
- They are not "aware" of the fact that the model of the world is itself in the world.

Machines therefore need people to:

- Keep them aligned to context.
- Keep them stable given the variability and change inherent in the world.
- Repair their ontologies.
- Keep the model aligned with the world.

People are not limited in that:

- Sensitivity to context is high and is knowledge- and attention-driven.
- Sensitivity to change is high and is driven by the recognition of anomaly.
- Adaptability to change is high and is goal-driven.
- They are aware of the fact that the model of the world is itself in the world.

Yet they create machines to:

- Help them stay informed of ongoing events.
- Help them align and repair their perceptions because they rely on mediated stimuli.
- Effect positive change following situation change.
- Computationally instantiate their models of the world.

As is the case in much of the world, this second list is more complicated, less memetic, and more true. Take the design of air-traffic control systems as an example. We cannot just trust the system to track planes, having it tap a human on the shoulder when there's a problem, which is what the HABA-MABA list implies. Instead, we have to create tools for monitoring the skies, helping the controllers manage their attention and overcome vigilance limitations, and select quickly from reasonable contingency plans when things go poorly.

If you are new to the practice of designing for agents, disabuse yourself of the freshman mistake of thinking you can just assign computer-type tasks to the computers and be done with it.

It's About the Feedback

In the 1940s and 1950s, a handful of systems thinkers established the field of *cybernetics*, which is about—to quote the subtitle of Norbert Wiener's 1948 book directly—*Control and Communication in the Animal and the Machine*. More specifically, they investigated systems that work by feedback loops to stabilize toward some goal. The thermostat, which you'll recall is the example that opens this book, is a common example and subject of study, but they also looked at many other systems, like the biochemical systems that regulate human body chemistry, how an animal adapts its behavior over time, even the behavior of mentally disturbed patients. Over time, they came to study more and more general systems, including consciousness itself.

Cybernetician William Ross Ashby even invented a machine, first described in his book *Design for a Brain*, called a *homeostat*. This machine featured a set of four floating magnets, the positions of which a user could interfere with using a set of potentiometers, but which would always return to a stable position. It demonstrated some of the key concepts of *feedback* and *ultrastability*.

Although the field of cybernetics is far-reaching and abstract enough, its texts read a bit like alchemy; one of the key concepts they formalized is that systems that are able to stabilize themselves rely on feedback for correction. Imagine trying to steer a boat toward some point on the horizon. Given the flow of water under the boat and the wind around the boat, it's quite likely you can't aim the boat directly, but have to offset your steering to compensate for these forces and keep adjusting as they change. That requires feedback and adaptation, and that's cybernetics.

Certainly, the engineers developing agentive systems will have their hands full of feedback as they ensure that the technology works toward the user's goals, but these loops will also be some of the key use cases by which users tailor agentive technology first to their own goals and preferences, and later to changes in those goals and the circumstances of use. It would be nice if we could implement technology so perfectly that it would never need correction and could just be trusted to do the right thing always, but until that magical time occurs, we're in the business of helping it adapt and learn. As you'll see in the next section, users will want to monitor the performance of agents and correct their false negatives and false positives. This will rarely be as easy as that simple sentence might make it seem.

Agency Is Fluid

In his 2013 article "The Seven Deadly Myths of Autonomous Systems," Jeffrey Bradshaw and his coauthors discussed some similarly tempting-but-wrong concepts. For example, it's tempting to think of agents as a widget—something you just add into an existing workflow. But as you saw earlier, that's not how it works. The agent *changes* the nature of the tasks of which it is a part.

Or it's tempting to think of agency within a system as a switch that gets turned on or off when necessary. But the humans involved with agentive systems will be unpracticed and unprepared to take over a system that suddenly loses an agentive member. (More about this in Chapter 9, "Handoff and Takeback.")

Perhaps the most nefarious is the notion that there are levels of autonomy that progress from one to the other, as embodied in the 2000 paper by Raja Parasuraman et al., "A Model for Types and Levels of Human Interaction with Automation." Those levels follow. Each line describes the tool as one of the following:

- **Fully manual**
- Showing the user every option
- Narrowing the options
- Suggesting the "best"
- Asking the user to approve an action

- Giving the user time to veto a selected action

- Keeping the user informed of actions that have been taken

- Responding to user inquiry about actions that have been taken

- Deciding when to inform the user of actions that have been taken

- **Fully autonomous**

I list them because they're fine examples of ways that software might help its users and as such, are worth considering, even when most of them are assistive rather than agentive. Certainly, check them out and consider them in your projects. But I describe the list as a whole as *nefarious* because it *seems* reasonable, yet has many problems. Rather than trying to deconstruct this list myself, I'll instead summarize the objections provided by R. Murphy et al., in a 2012 report for the Department of Defense, "The Role of Autonomy in DoD Systems," who wrote their paper specifically to challenge its continued use.

They note that it's far from complete. There are nuances between these levels, and possibilities outside of the scope of *decision* and *action selection*. The list does not admit that a given agent may be "low" in self-sufficiency but "high" in self-directedness. It implies that all types of work undertaken by an agent would be set at the same level, although this is not true. It implies that aspects of a system that could involve agency would be set at the same level, although this is not true. It doesn't take into account that different tasks and contexts undertaken by the same agent may require different approaches. Lastly, most of the challenges being faced by the DoD in terms of (2012) agency are around user-centered teamwork, and the model does not help with any aspect of that.

A better model is to do away with thinking of agency as having levels. It is better to think of the workflows, goals, and tasks of the individual or team, and then build agentive (or assistive) tools that enable mutual observability, predictability, and directability. Think of agency as fluid. If you are more interested in this line of thinking, be sure to check out the corresponding paper published a year later by Johnson et al., "Seven Cardinal Virtues of Human-Machine Teamwork: Examples from the DARPA Robotic Challenge."

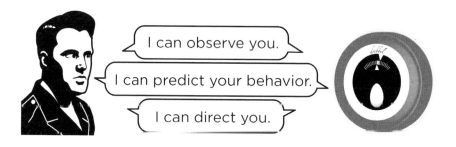

The Agentive/Assistive Line Will Be Blurry

In their 2004 paper, "Six Modes of Proactive Resource Management: A User-Centric Typology for Proactive Behaviors," Antti Salovaara and Antti Oulasvirta of the Helsinki Institute for Information Technology shared six use cases, which could be used to brainstorm applications of narrow AI.

- **Preparation:** Can objects and places know when people are headed their way and prepare themselves for use? Think of a projector warming itself before the presenter arrives.

- **Optimization:** Can the agent observe available possibilities and pick the right one for the user's goals? Think of your smartphone picking between cellular data, Wi-Fi, and Bluetooth, as the circumstances need.

- **Advising:** Can agents observe tasks in progress and suggest better or alternate options? Think of Waze and Google Maps suggesting new traffic routes to riders behind a freeway accident.

- **Manipulation:** What can the agent do on its own when it is absolutely certain it is what the user wants? Think of Gmail creating an item on your calendar when an email clearly describes it to a recipient.

- **Inhibition:** Can the agent understand enough of the context to know what is welcome and suppress the rest? Think of presentation software that suppresses notifications that would distract your audience.

- **Finalization:** What can the agent end or close when it is no longer in use? Think of your phone or desktop going to "sleep" to save on energy.

These ideas are useful for thinking about what agentive technology might do. For purposes of this point, though, note that this list blends assistive modes, as with advising, and agentive modes. In the products I've designed and workshops I've run, it's been clear that only very simple agents will be purely agentive or purely assistive. Sophisticated products will move between these modes, depending on the confidence of their algorithms, the context, and user needs.

Recap: On the Agentive Shoulders of Giants

Part of my task in writing this book is to introduce practitioners to the legacy of deep academic thought around the topic of agents and agentive technology, so you can be well-equipped as you begin to formalize your practice around it as well. This chapter lists major learnings, but is far from exhaustive. There are other fantastic insights to be had throughout the publications and documented talks of automation and agents. I quote more in the course of the text where they are relevant.

PART II

Doing

The prior part was a persuasive argument, with considerations that were largely strategic and futurist: Going deep into a singular example before coming back up for air to examine what makes agentive tech interesting and valuable across lots of examples, and then wrapping it all up with a history of the concepts involved in agentive design. And now, presuming you are duly persuaded that you need to get on this bandwagon, *stat*, let's shift gears. It may be a bit jarring, because we're going from designing the *right thing* to designing the *thing right*.

In this section, I want to look pragmatically at what it means to design for this technology. What are the new tools we have to design with? What are the new use cases and scenarios? How do we evaluate the success of an agent? Though this technology is building steam in the consumer space and the practice of designing for it emerging, this section should be a useful starting point for anyone beginning to think about, design for, and build in the medium.

CHAPTER 5

A Modified Frame for Interaction

O ver the next handful of chapters, we'll be reviewing some use cases that are particular to agentive technology. Understanding them is easier when we compare how the broad model of interaction changes when you start thinking agentively, and that involves rethinking the see-think-do loop.

A New See-Think-Do Loop

Most computer-related fields have some version of the following diagram. Lisanne Bainbridge calls it *"Monitor → Diagnose → Operate"* with academically appropriate Latinate language. Computer programming texts refer to it from the computer's perspective as *"Input → Processing → Output."* I prefer the simplicity of the Germanic labels *"See → Think → Do."* We know it's a vast oversimplification of the way cognition actually works, but it's a *useful* simplification of the interaction that a user has with a system. If this sounds very abstract and basic, that's where its instructive power comes from. Let's look at the loop from a traditional model of the user as a *task-doer*.

Consider a person walking into a dark room. She *sees* that the room is dark → *thinks* that she could find her keys there more easily with more light → *flips the light switch* to on. This is a very basic task and a very simple scenario. More commonly, scenarios are made of many see-think-do loops in succession.

To be precise, "see" is more appropriately "sense," since our user can hear an audible alarm or feel the rumble of haptic feedback, but "see" is more commonly true and more memetic than "perceive," so let's stick to "see."

The loop can describe interactions at many levels. It could, for example, describe microinteractions.

Andrés **reads** "Please select" in the "State" field → **thinks** that it should be Arizona → **clicks** on the drop-down control to open the list of state abbreviations...

The loop describes a person using some *thing*, and that *thing* has its own mirror image as it responds to what the person does. This responder could be a person who is hearing, thinking, and responding in a conversation with the other, but more to our purposes, that responder is most often a computer system, which as noted previously will respond with a loop of *input* → *processing* → *output*. In the following "bow tie" diagram, the computer's loop is added to the human's loop and colored blue to distinguish it. Together these two form something of a lemniscate, or infinity symbol, describing the back-and-forth of interactive systems.

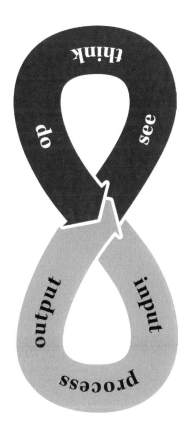

We can apply this simple, powerful structure to narrow AI to see how things will change. With *assistive* technologies, in which a narrow AI helps a person perform some task, the diagram is no longer just a human on one side and a computer system on the other. There's an additional computer line on top, flowing right alongside the human, while the human does the heavy lifting of seeing, thinking, and doing. The computer might be helping to materialize information or draw attention to particular information (see), doing some of the calculations, modeling alternate scenarios, or recommending a best-guess next course of action (think), acting as an interpreter to complex APIs, managing messaging across a network of recipients, or enacting commands through a network of actuators (doing). Notably, the person is always the primary problem solver, with the agent augmenting and supporting them. This augmented-human idea isn't new. It goes at least as far back as 1960, when J.C.R. Licklider described such a system as "Man-Computer Symbiosis."

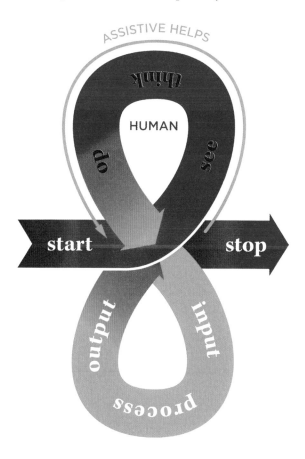

When we shift from an assistive to an *agentive* perspective, the graph changes to show the computer system doing the heavy lifting, with a human poking in occasionally. The agent may perform some of the same tasks, but only share it with the user when the task is complete or when asked. Note also that where using a tool might have a definite beginning and definite ending, an agent often operates indefinitely, and so has less start and stop, and more setup and disengagement. While this graphic doesn't have much of an explanatory system on its own, it is a structure on which we can hang and understand the scenarios that are new to agentive systems; it's a helpful organizing principle for discussing the differences in what they can do.

The use cases we'll look at over the next few chapters can be understood as originating in one of these activities.

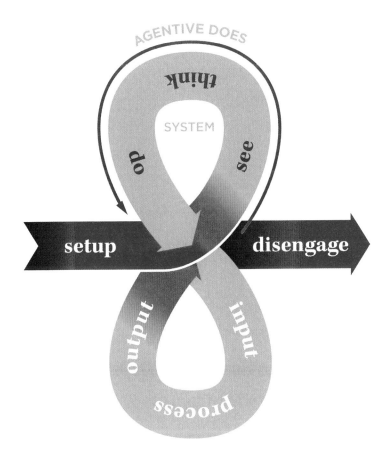

Setting Up the Agent

- Understanding the agent's capabilities and limitations.
- Conveying your goals and preferences.
- Granting your permissions and authorization.
- Taking the agent out for a test drive.
- Launching the agent.
- Discovering and adding new capabilities as they come available or grow popular.

Seeing What the Agent Is Doing

- Monitoring what's happening.
- Receiving notifications of successes and problems.

Having or Helping the Agent Do Stuff

- Pausing and restarting the agent.
- Playing alongside the agent.
- Tuning triggers and behaviors such that they perform better in the future.
- Handing off the task to some intermediate person, or even a different, non-human actor.
- Practicing the main task to maintain skills.
- Taking over the task from the agent.
- Handing the task back to the agent.

Disengaging from the Agent

- The user's no longer needing the agent.
- The user's passing.

You may note that "thinking" is missing from the previous headers. That's partly because as far as the user's experience is concerned, the thinking that an agent does while it's working routinely is a black box, something mostly for developers to worry about. It is during this process, though, that the agent will not just be processing next steps, but also learning and improving.

Rules and Exceptions, Triggers and Behaviors

While tuning the agent, users will run into the rules by which they operate, and the exceptions when they should not. For some agents, this will be as simple as setting a time to run each day. For more complicated agents, it may involve rules, made up of *triggers*, by which an agent knows it's time for action, and *behaviors*, which guide how that action is performed. Agents have to help their users as they try and do this tuning, which is at its essence constrained programming, even though they are likely to be utterly unfamiliar with the arcane requirements of real programming. We'll discuss these in more detail—including an example built around music—in Chapter 8, "Handling Exceptions."

New Technologies to Consider

One of the fun things we get to consider when dealing with artificial intelligence is that in order to enable it to carry out its seeing, thinking, and doing duties, we must include cutting-edge technologies in the system. Trying to list these authoritatively is something of a fool's errand, because by the time the book is published, some will have already fallen out of use or become unremarkable, and there will be some new ones to consider. Also, I wouldn't pretend to have collected a complete list. But by understanding them in terms of seeing, thinking, and doing, we can more quickly understand their purpose for an agent, and thereby the user. We can also begin to think in terms of these building blocks when designing agentive technologies—to have them in our backpack. We can also have a frame for contextualizing future technologies as they become available. So, at the risk of providing lists that are just too cursory, I've built the following based on existing APIs, notably IBM's Watson and a bit of Microsoft's Cognitive Services.

Seeing

The agent needs to be able to sense everything it needs in order to perform its job at least as well as the user, and in many cases, in ways the user can't sense. While many of these sensing technologies seem simple and unremarkable for a human, teaching a computer to do these things is a remarkable achievement in and of itself, and very useful to equip agents to do their jobs.

- **Object recognition:** Enables a computer to identify objects present in an image or video feed.

- **Face recognition:** Helps a computer identify a person with computer recognition of their facial features.

- **Biometrics:** Helps identify a person through physical metrics. There are dozens of biometric technologies including fingerprints, voice prints, and even the unique pattern of capillaries in the eyes or just beneath the surface of the face. Biometrics can assist other higher-order algorithms, such as heart rate, helping convey stress in affective computing.

- **Gaze monitoring:** Helps the computer determine where the people around it are looking, and inferring intention, context, and even pragmatic meaning from it.

- **Natural language processing:** Allows the user to give instructions or ask questions of a computer in everyday language. The algorithm can also identify keywords, unique phrases, and high-level concepts in a given text.

- **Voice recognition:** Computer parses the messy sounds of human speech into language.

- **Handwriting recognition:** User inputs data and instructions through handwritten text.

- **Sentiment:** Computer determines the pragmatic sense of a text; whether it is positive or negative, or even whether the speaker is being ironic.

- **Gesture recognition:** Computer interprets the meanings conveyed through body positions and motions.

- **Activity recognition:** Computer infers what activities a person is engaging in, and it changes modes to accommodate the different activities. A simple example is helping computers understand that people need to sleep, and recognizing when this is happening and know that its behavior should change during this time.

- **Affect recognition:** Computer infers a user's emotional state from a variety of inputs such as the tone of their voice, their gestures, or their facial expressions.

- **Personality insights:** Simply moving through a connected world and participating in social media, we tell a lot about ourselves and our opinions, interests, and problems. If a user gives an agent permission to access these digital trails, much of the user's goals, personality and frustrations can be inferred, saving them the trouble of having to tell the agent explicitly.

The Coming Flood of Inferences

Much of this list of sensing technologies feels intuitive and what a human might call "direct." For instance, you can observe a transcript of what I just told my phone, and point to the keywords by which it understood that I wanted it to set a 9-minute timer. In fact, it's not direct at all; it's a horribly complicated ordeal to get to that transcript, but it feels so easy to us that we think of it as direct.

But there is vastly more data that can be *inferred* from direct data. For instance, most people balk at the notion that the government has access to actual recordings of their telephone conversations, but much less so about their phone's metadata, that is, the numbers that were called, what order they were called, and how long the conversations were.

Yet in 2016, Jonathan Mayer, Patrick Mutchler, and John C. Mitchell of Stanford University published a study titled "Evaluating the Privacy Properties of Telephone Metadata." In it they wrote that narrow AI software that analyzed test subjects' phone metadata, and using some smart heuristics, was able to determine some deeply personal things about them, such as that one was likely suffering from cardiac arrhythmia, and that another owned a semi-automatic rifle. The personal can be inferred from the impersonal.

Similarly, it's fairly common practice for web pages to watch what you're doing, where you've come from, and what it knows you've done in the past to break users into demographic and psychographic segments. If you've liked a company in the past and visit their site straight from an advertising link that's gone viral, you're in a different bucket than the person who goes to their page after having gone to Consumer Reports, and the site adjusts itself accordingly.

These two examples show that in addition to whatever data we could get from direct sensing technologies, we can expect much, much more data from inference engines.

Thinking

Though largely the domain of artificial intelligence engineering, it's interesting to know what goes into the sophisticated processing of artificial intelligence. To a lesser extent, these can inform design of these systems, although collaboration with developers actually working on the agentive system is the best way to understand real-world capabilities and constraints.

- **Domain expertise:** Grants an agent an ontological model of the domain in which it acts. This can be as simple as awareness of the calendar or a fixed pattern for sweeping a floor, or as complex as thermodynamics.

- **Common-sense engines:** Encode a body of knowledge that most people would regard as readily apparent about the world, such as that "a rose is a plant" and that "all plants need water to live." Although people consider such things unremarkable, computers must be taught them explicitly.

- **Reasoners/inference engines:** Make use of common-sense engines, the semantic web, and natural language parsing to make inferences about the world such as "a rose needs water to live" from the givens above.

- **Predictive algorithms:** Allow a computer to predict within a range of confidence variable outcomes based on a set of givens, and act according to its confidence in a particular outcome happening.

- **Machine learning:** Enables a computer to identify patterns in data, as well as improve its performance of a task to be more effective toward a goal.

- **Trade-off analytics:** Can make a recommendation for users balancing multiple objectives, even with many factors.

- **Prediction:** By comparing individual cases against past examples, algorithms can predict what will likely happen next. This can be as small as the next letters in an incomplete word, next words in an incomplete sentence, or as large as what a user is likely to do or take interest in next.

Doing

- **Screens:** Let agents convey graphic information.

- **Messages:** Let agents convey textual information, often to a user's mobile devices.

- **Sound:** Lets agents convey information audibly.

- **Speech synthesis:** Lets agents generate human-sounding speech for conversational output.

- **Haptic actuators:** Let agents generate touch sensations. The vibrator in your smartphone is one example, and the rumble pack in video game console controllers is another.

- **Robotics:** Let agents control a physical device precisely. This can be as "simple" as the appliances in a home to something as complicated as car-manufacturing robot arms on a factory floor, or something as nuanced as conveying information and emotion through expression.

- **Drones:** Let agents control a mobile robot, whether swimming, driving, flying, or propelling through space.

- **APIs:** Allow computers to interact with other computer systems and other agents, passing information, requests, or responses back and forth, including across the world via the internet, and across the room through short-distance wireless.

Handling a Range of Complexity

We're about to look at a collection of use cases to consider when designing agentive technology in the next chapters. Please note that I tried to be comprehensive, which means there are a lot. But your agent may only need a few, or not even any. Consider one of my favorite examples, the Garden Defense Electronic Owl. It has a switch to turn it on, and thereafter it turns its scary owl face toward detected motion and hoots. That's all it does, and all it needs to do. If you're building something that simple, you won't need to study setup patterns or worry how it might hand its responsibilities off to a human collaborator.

Simpler agents may involve a handful of these patterns, and highly sophisticated, mission-critical agents may involve all of these and more. It is up to you to understand which one of these use cases applies to your particular agent.

Recap: New Tools in Your Backpack

Designing systems that act on behalf of their users—rather than building smart tools for users to operate—requires some new approaches compared to traditional product design.

- You must reconceive *see-think-do* loops with the computer system doing the heavy lifting and the human's occasional involvement.

- This fact means that there are new use cases to consider when designing scenarios. (More on these in subsequent chapters.)

- You must keep abreast of new technologies that allow the agent to do its seeing, thinking, and doing.

Agentive Gardening with Mr. McGregor

Introduction

Part of the point of this book is that agentive technology is on the rise, and because of this, I only have about two-dozen, easy-to-convey examples on hand. (See Appendix B, "A List of Referenced Agentive Technology," for the full list I referenced while writing.) Since I refer to examples quite a lot over the course of this section to illustrate some abstract points, those examples can feel repetitive because, well, they are. It would be good to have another example to focus on.

Additionally, it would be nice to have an example that we could consider as if we were a product team working with agentive concepts. This is the perspective I expect that you, the reader, have, and so such an example would be instructive.

To these ends, let's consider a speculative product called *Mr. McGregor*. You may recognize the name as the cranky, Scottish gardener from the Beatrix Potter books about Peter Rabbit. This product *will* be about gardening, and less about crankiness and rabbit pie. The purpose here is not to design such a system to a real level of detail, but rather to illustrate how thinking agentively helps take some of the workload off the user. Here I will lay out the basics of the product, and then follow some chapters in Part II by applying its lessons to this example.

For this imaginary product, our client is an established brick-and-mortar gardening store called *Potter* in Austin that wants to offer a leading-edge product to deepen their relationship with their most loyal clients. Potter has never been in the software space before, but they're excited by the opportunity to offer a differentiator. They like using the Mr. McGregor character since it ties into their brand, which is built around Peter Rabbit. They've come to us to help them envision what this agentive product could be.

It will be useful to have a persona to speak about as we discuss Mr. McGregor. Since this is a toy problem written up for the sake of illustration, let's use an abbreviated description.

Chuck

Having just moved next to his sister, Kate, who is a lifelong gardener, Chuck has become inspired to take up gardening for himself. The trouble is, he has a brown thumb, a busy schedule, and a lot of pride. He's not going to ask her, and needs a lot of help to keep up. That's where Mr. McGregor can step in to help.

Here are Chuck's goals:

- Have a gorgeous garden he can show off to his sister.
- Have fresh veggies and herbs on hand for cooking.
- Keep costs and time spent gardening to a minimum.

If this were a real design challenge, we'd need to know a lot more about the givens, but for our purposes this is enough: We want to create an agentive gardening product, thinking of Chuck and Potter's admittedly loosely defined business goals.

About Chuck's Name

In 2016, librarian George Dore and library assistant Scott Amey grew frustrated that the agentive demand-driven acquisitions software in charge of optimizing their library's collection might remove important books. For example, no one was checking out Steinbeck's *Cannery Row*, so the librarians feared that the algorithm was going to remove it. They had no way to "bless" titles as untouchable. To guard against algorithmic tyranny, the two created a fictional patron, Chuck Finley, who would borrow books to bolster that book's numbers in the database and thereby protect it.

We cannot be slavish to use-algorithms. They can create dangerous positive-feedback loops and echo chambers. I believe this is especially true at institutions whose purpose is the preservation of cultural capital, like museums and libraries. For this reason, I heartily applaud Dore and Amey's hack.

Unfortunately, some whistleblower reported them, and among other repercussions, Chuck Finley was erased from the East Lake County Library's roster. But in honor of their hack, I've christened this book's persona with the same name. Long live Chuck Finley.[1]

Avoid pushing your users into a similar corner with the "Add to a Whitelist" pattern described in Chapter 8.

---

1 http://www.heraldnet.com/news/to-save-books-librarians-created-their -own-fictional-reader/

Chuck's Yard

He lives in Austin, Texas, in a one-story home in a suburb with a low fenced-in backyard that's about 12 meters square and looks out onto a district park. A patch of lawn takes up about half the space. There is a raised bed near the southeast wall. A mature Meyer Lemon tree is—when he moves in—the only food-bearing plant.

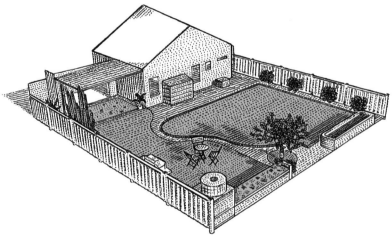

MODIFIED "MARICOPA BACKYARD" BY USER "MARICOPA HOUSE,"
MODIFIED "PINEWOOD COLLECTION" FENCE BY USER "CHRIS T." SKETCHUP 3D WAREHOUSE

Mr. McGregor Components

The agent can work on the cheap with no additional components, prompting users to be its eyes, ears, and hands for its part of the work. But to show off what agentive (and future) tech can do, we'll say Chuck has some extra money and is a bit of a gadget nerd, so he would purchase several optional components, especially if they promised to take the burden off of him.

- Ground thermometers

- Soil moisture sensors

- Zone-controlled drip irrigation system

- Wall-mounted wide-angle Wi-Fi camera

Agentive Gardening with Mr. McGregor

The Bee

Chuck is most enamored of a small drone called the "Bee" that Mr. McGregor can use for a variety of purposes. The drone has a camera that can see in the infrared spectrum and has a wall-mountable charging base.

- It routinely takes photos of the plants to check for growth and damage.
- It uses the built-in camera continuously while the drone is charging.

We'll see more detail of these ideas later in the book, but this is just a taste to illustrate why it should be an option in the product. There are lots of genuine uses for it. It's not hard to imagine a drone that could even deliver things like pellets of fertilizer or micro sprays of pesticide, but might push us too far into *autonomy* to exercise the patterns we want to be working with. For now, let's just say it has the camera.

Data Sources

The agent will rely on several data sources.

- Mr. McGregor servers
- Clock
- Calendars
- Gardening databases
- Weather and Almanac services
- APIs for local services like pest control or arborists
- The sensors in Chuck's smartphone (with permission)
- Chuck's social media (with permission)

Look for similar sidebars later in the book as we consider the agentive design of Mr. McGregor.

CHAPTER 6

Ramping Up
with an Agent

A few agents operate in a small enough domain that there's very little to no setup, but more sophisticated, powerful, and interesting agents will require conscious attention to setting them up to perform well. There are five key aspects to design:

- Conveying capability
- Conveying limitations
- Getting goals, preferences, and permissions
- Test driving
- Launch

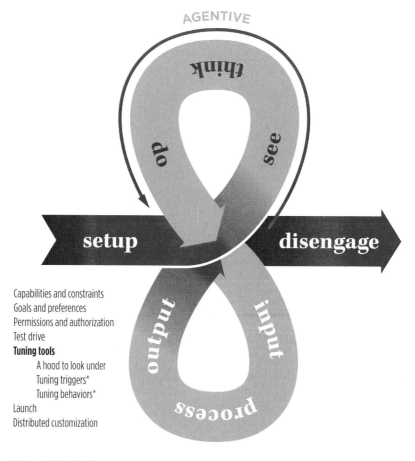

Capabilities and constraints
Goals and preferences
Permissions and authorization
Test drive
Tuning tools
    A hood to look under
    Tuning triggers*
    Tuning behaviors*
Launch
Distributed customization

* Discussed in Chapter 8

Conveying Capability

New and potential users need to understand what a given agent can do. Marketing, advertising, and product placement are ways you can convey capability in mass media. A well-crafted name and tagline can make its purpose easy to understand, recall, and convey.

The agent itself presents another set of possibilities.

When physical agents like the Roomba vacuum are active, their capability may be obvious. *Ah, I see, it vacuums.* When these agents are dormant, their industrial design may provide some clues. Any physical controls can convey capability if they are well-labeled.

Digital agents will have an even greater challenge to convey capability for being immaterial and not having physical affordances. Actual use can be conveyed in two ways.

First, if results are shared on social media, you can have hooks back to the product or engender conversations with friends curious about the agent. For example, when Narrative posts to your Facebook wall, it includes a little link where you can learn more about Narrative. Some agents won't have a social media component (who wants their Roomba to tweet every time it cleans your floors?), and sometimes that link will be seen as overaggressive marketing. But sometimes just the results themselves can start a conversation. "Hey, Chris, how did you get these pictures of the party? I didn't see a camera in your hand the whole evening!" On the plus side, social media alerts can be part of how the user knows that the agent is still running.

A second way to convey capability through use is via a trial run, where users get to just try it out and see for themselves. More on that later, since it's very similar to the trial run that committed users might want to try during setup.

Conveying Limitations

Given that agentive tech is, by definition, not a general artificial intelligence, a key thing to convey is what *it can't do*, so users don't approach it with expectations that are too high and subsequently feel let down. Marketing, brand, and industrial design will be your users' first impressions, and they serve as major clues.

It's my opinion that attempts at anthropomorphization should be avoided or undertaken with great caution. The biggest temptation is to use human language, perhaps because it's easier than, say, creating a believable human face. But conversational, first-person language raises expectations that narrow AI can't meet. When Siri asks, "What can I help you with?" I'd expect it to handle anything, including, "Well, I'd like to know if there's been any research into what signals trigger an intentional stance in an observer, but I'm not sure of the search terms." Rather than some sympathetic response like, "I'm not sure that exists, but I'll look into it and get back to you." Instead it kind of stares at me dumbly afterward saying, "I'm not sure I understand." Which is, frankly, more frustrating.

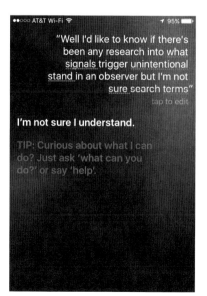
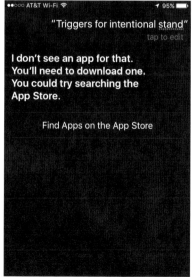

If it instead said something dumber like, "Command?" it would appear less capable, and I wouldn't be tempted to try complex queries. I'd be more likely to say "search for triggers for intentional stance" and, when it prompts me to search the app store, I would be less frustrated because my expectations weren't that high to begin with.

So more-constrained or even zoomorphic signals are better alternatives to start with. These convey capabilities that are less-than-human, a better fit for the actual capabilities of narrow AI, and may even earn a bit of sympathy from users when the agent runs into trouble.

Getting Goals, Preferences, and Permissions

Agents will have the *ultimate* goal of their use predefined. Spotify, for instance, is for listening to music and not much else. The Nest Thermostat is for controlling temperature. Roomba is for cleaning floors. No one needs to clarify for their Roomba that it does not need to concern itself with music selection for the household.

Smart Defaults

To encourage initial adoption, the amount of setup for any agent should be kept to a minimum. Providing smart defaults is a good way to have an agent work *well enough*, even if the user declines to provide specifics. It's a fair bet, for example, that most people in the United States will aim for a retirement age of 66 or 67 since this is the earliest that the law supports full benefits, so if that's an important piece of data for your agent, you can set that as a default and let the user correct it if necessary.

While agents should be designed to run with smart defaults, setting up an agent's subgoals and preferences of how the agent is to do its work is important. This can be handled implicitly or explicitly.

Implicitly

Another way to minimize the amount of setup data is to gather what you need implicitly. People leave more and more digital trails as they move through the world, and those trails can provide a lot of data if you can parse it. Social media is one obvious category. From Twitter, for instance, you can infer users' language preferences, attitudes about the things they write about, and even the times they're typically awake. Users who grant access to their Facebook accounts are sharing that information and the interests they've indicated in their profiles.

Private data is another source of implicit information, if the user grants permission. If a music recommender agent can see your current digital music collection, it will have a very good idea of what your tastes are, presuming you collect music you enjoy (rather than, say, collecting for study). Designers should be careful to only ask permission if it's absolutely necessary, as it can come across as invasive. When you do it, explain why you're asking by explaining the benefits.

Another way to implicitly convey preferences is to have the agent watch how a task is currently being performed. For example, your driving agent could watch you drive a few times to note how heavily you accelerate and break, or what the minimum distance you maintain behind other cars is, in order to understand these variables for its own settings. The Nest Thermostat pays attention to how users adjust temperature to refine its model.

Explicitly

Sometimes it's not possible to pick up on settings implicitly. Perhaps the risks of getting it wrong are too great, or it is not legally permissible. For these cases, you'll need the users to provide their settings explicitly. That data can be specific, like particular calendar dates, but agent settings are commonly abstract rules and exceptions. This is because agents are very often persistent. You can set the Roomba to clean a floor once manually, but more often than not, it is performing the task on a routine basis. This means there is a *rule* for it to follow. For instance, the Roomba rule might be set to run every afternoon, except on the weekends.

A rule is a collection of *triggers* and *exceptions*, connected to a set of *actions* and *constraints*. If you're familiar with If This…Then That, then you're familiar with this structure since this is their whole model and, yes, their name.

Triggers can be thought of as specifying when the actions should be taken, but they aren't just date/time stamps. They can include the state of any variable the agent knows about: temperature out of a range, keywords spoken, emails received, biometric data within a range, or the number of cat videos posted to YouTube this week. Some agents won't need exceptions, but I'd guess most agents will need them.

Once the trigger is met, the agent needs to know what it is to do next. Sometimes the action is fixed, such as the Narrative taking a picture or Roomba's vacuuming the floor. If not, the action and its variables need to be specified. *Text me. Contact the nearest police officer. Feed my dog.* Constraints to the action help avoid the Sorcerer's Apprentice problem. (You'll remember those innumerable brooms walking around the hapless apprentice, toting water, as described in Chapter 4, "Six Takeaways from the History of Agentive Thinking.") Not all actions need it, but for the examples listed earlier in the paragraph, it's easy to see what those constraints might be. Text me *up to a maximum of three times per day.* Contact the nearest police officer *who is not currently on a case.* Feed my dog *up to a maximum of two bowls per day, even if she's whining for more and gives you the sad puppy eyes.*

Whatever tools you provide for the user to explicitly establish the rules, they should follow good form design principles, since it is a task of providing data. More and more agents let users complete this setup on their phones or computers and then pipe that data to their individual agent.

As long as we're in the world of narrow AI, it's worth noting that the interfaces by which users convey their preferences can be a graphic user interface, or they could be conversational, using a natural language interface or NLI. In fact, some people use "agent" to refer to this kind of input, which can be a little confusing since the user's attention is on them, so they're assistive. Natural language is very powerful as an input since people are generally comfortable and relatively good at using language to express themselves and their needs. That said, I hope designers will be careful about not overusing this kind of interface, as a graphic output can be much more understandable to users when reviewing a set of options than a string of text.

Test Driving

If the risks are small, an agent can just launch. The worst that could happen with Spotify is the user might hear a song she doesn't enjoy. But some agents need to be test driven, so users can get a feel for how it will perform, to build enough trust before launch. For example, an investor might want to see how a roboinvestor would perform with a portfolio of fake money and the user's preferences. If it performs favorably enough, then give it real money to manage. If it doesn't, they will need tools for tuning the rules in real time (see Chapter 7, "Everything Running Smoothly," for more on tuning.)

Users will want to monitor the test drive, so you may need to have the agent work in a more compressed schedule than it might ordinarily work, or act on demand even if the trigger conditions aren't met. No investor wants to wait a year to see how the roboinvestor might perform across the year.

Users additionally need *a hood to look under,* meaning a way to find out why the agent made the decisions it made. After all, it might have made the right decision for the wrong reason, or just barely made a decision the user would have chosen strongly. It's another opportunity for the user to tune the rules before launch. What is revealed "under the hood" depends on the particular agent, but one solution is the constrained natural language tools described in Chapter 8, "Handling Exceptions."

The test drive is also a way for a user to get to know the limitations of the agent, or what David Rose calls the "guardrail experience" in his book *Enchanted Objects.* What can it do? What can't it do? What will it need help with? Rose tells how the designers of Siri anticipated this setup behavior when you tell it, *"Siri, I love you,"* and it responds, *"I value you."* It's a clever way to convey the limitations of the product and tell the users that designers have anticipated even their playful use.

Launch

After the user is convinced that the agent is set up well and can be trusted to do its job, it's time to launch.

While a tool might just warrant a simple button click, if the setup of an agent has taken some investment of time, effort, or money—or even the benefits of using the agent are expected to be high—launch might warrant a bit more of a fanfare, a celebration that the agent is live.

Furthermore, if the agent is live but patiently waiting for its trigger, the user needs some sense that even though it looks idle, it is, in fact, on task. Including a bit of monitoring feedback should help the user understand that. For instance, if the agent is waiting for a particular moment in time, show a timer patiently counting down. If it's measuring temperature, show the current temp and visualize the threshold temp. If it's monitoring sounds, show a small soundwave.

Lastly, just as when you learn to ski and the first thing they teach you is how to fall down and get back up, one of the first things the user should be able to tell after launch is how to pause and resume the agent. This could be a glowing red button, or it could be the magic keywords it needs to speak, but it will reassure your user she hasn't just let loose something she can't control.

It is likely that the user will check in frequently in the beginning to make sure that things are on track. Keep the monitoring feedback running and use the opportunity to collect some of the things you skipped in setup. For instance, this pre-run is a good time to float customization options. But you might also push them after launch, as discussed next.

Distributed Customization

It is tempting to try and get everything set up before use actually starts, but since agentive technology plays out over time, you can delay optional customization until later. This will help keep the setup scenarios simpler and give the agent a legitimate reason to get back in touch with the user during early use—even if everything is going fine—helping to keep the agent top-of-mind without resorting to bald-faced spam.

For one roboinvestor I worked on, the design team knew that having investors visualize their goals was a positive, persuasive technique that helped them stick to their plan over the long haul. We wanted them to select or upload a picture for each goal they had, like buying a new home, saving for retirement, or sending a child to college. Do you want a reminder of why you're making the sacrifices you are? Here's a picture of graduation caps in the air. Imagine that one will belong to your kid.

We could have had them select these images during setup when they were creating their financial goals, but we wanted to keep it down to as short a time as possible. So we pushed it off until a few weeks after the launch of the roboinvestor. This way, it wouldn't add to the setup, and since it was going to be its own "event," we could take a little more time in explaining why it was a good thing to do and even help the investor along the process. Had we tried to squeeze it into the setup scenario, there would have been pressures to make it faster and more efficient.

Recap: Ramping Up Is Often the Tedious Part

Simple, single-purpose agents can just be turned on and let go. But for more sophisticated agents, getting started will be the hard part. As product managers, designers, and developers, your job is to take this into consideration and work to make these scenarios as smooth and as smart as possible. Consider these questions for the agentive technology you're working on.

- **Conveying capabilities and limitations:** Help your user learn what the agentive technology can and cannot do.

- **Understanding your user's goals and preferences:** Specify how the agent learns what the user wants to accomplish and how they want it accomplished.

- **Permissions and authorizations:** Help the agent build trust and get permission to access the information that will help the agent do its job.

- **Test driving:** Give the user the opportunity to give the agent a trial run, to make sure that it is set up well and will work as intended.

- **Launch:** Build a launch mechanism that conveys trust and confidence in the agent.

Ramping Up

How would these patterns come into play for Chuck? Let's look at them each in turn and compare them to how the agent might work if you were thinking of it as a tool. It's the first time we will look at our example project in terms of the core idea of the book, so I'm going to lean in and touch on each one thoroughly. My hope is that here you see how at every step, the agent works to do what it can for Chuck, rather than providing tools for Chuck to do the step himself.

Conveying Capabilities and Limitations

Chuck would learn some of the capabilities and limitations of the agent when he first searched for a solution and found the Potter marketing web pages and any app reviews. But he couldn't rely just on that. What features might be apparent from using the product itself?

Given that the brand is a particular character, you would have to make a choice about anthropomorphizing Mr. McGregor. Does he appear as part of the product? Or is he just a logo? If he does appear, does the agent speak in his crotchety voice, or in a more neutral tone? Casting messages in his voice might raise the specter of an artificial intelligence more capable than what the service could actually deliver, so let's leave him as a decoration and adopt a neutral tone. This will give you more control over the language to explain the limitations and set Chuck's expectations.

Understanding Chuck's Goals, Settings, Preferences, and Permissions

If you were thinking of this as a gardening tool, you would perhaps design a few informative and usable forms for Chuck to read up on his options for gardening, a GUI for drawing a plan of his garden and specifying which crops he wanted to put where. Then he could go to the web app routinely to check on this model of his garden, review the tasks he needed to do, then go back and check them off when he had completed them to see the next steps.

But an agentive solution can do him so much better than that.

Inferring Chuck's Interest

In the agentive version, Chuck could grant Mr. McGregor access to his social media, which could prompt the agent to look around for clues to Chuck's interest in gardening. It would see what his friends and family were posting, and especially that his sister posted frequently about her own garden and the meals she made from the vegetables she grew, even complaints about deer in the neighborhood. His familial relationship to her and their adjacent addresses are major clues about the reasons that Chuck might be interested in gardening, so it's a high probability that home vegetable gardening would be a desire of his. So after he granted access to social media, the agent could tell him:

"I'm guessing you'd like to get into backyard vegetable gardening, right?"

By using artificial narrow intelligence and inference engines, you could provide smart defaults that made it easy for most users to simply say, *"Yes, that's right."*

Yes, That's Right

Mr. McGregor could do some smart inference on the content of what Chuck posted to social media, as well as when he did it, and infer that he worked quite a bit, so he wouldn't have much time to commit to gardening this first year.

"Does two hours each week sound like the right amount of time you'd like to spend?"

A tool would provide easy ways to do the work. An agent finds ways to do the work to the best of its ability and collaborates with the user to refine or correct it.

If Potter had partnered with something like the Soil Testing Lab at the University of Massachusetts, it could use those APIs to look into their databases. Did the previous owner do a soil sample for the yard? How long ago was it done? Have any neighbors done soil samples? If the data exists, this could be taken into consideration. If not, or it was a long time ago, Mr. McGregor could mention that it would be requesting a kit and ask if he wanted to wait for a few weeks for those results or begin without it. A tool might remind him to check the soil, but the agent could do it for him.

A follow-up question could ask Chuck what he'd be willing to spend on setting up his garden and what an ideal monthly budget might be. This would give the agent some resources to consider in the trade-offs of a successful garden, and come into play in a bit when you ask about the hardware. Chuck might not be comfortable connecting his bank account to the agent yet, but if he found it tedious, after he built trust, he might save his information to save himself the work.

Mr. McGregor could then pick some herbs and vegetables that fit Chuck's constraints and goals. They should have these qualifications:

- Be easy for a first-time gardener to grow.

- Take into consideration the "hardiness zone" of Austin and the microclimate of his yard next to the park.

- Be sure to include at least one crop that his sister grows so they have the opportunity to share experiences.

Planning the Layout

After Chuck has confirmed his goals, the agent could look at Google Maps for the satellite view of his address and make a first-draft map of his backyard that Chuck wouldn't need to build from scratch. He would just need to review it to correct it where it got things wrong.

Mr. McGregor could use some logic to divide up the areas he designated on the draft map into square-foot plots and pick a good arrangement of crops and herbs. A simple GUI could walk him through the apps' reasoning and let Chuck provide any missing information and corrections.

"These tomatoes will need plenty of sunlight," Mr. McGregor might tell him, *"so in this draft plan I put them near this warm, south-facing wall. Check and see if there might be anything that would cast a significant shadow over this spot. If so, we should pick a new place."*

More serious gardeners could work with an assistive tool to create a 3D model of the house and things around it to create a sunlight and shadow time-lapse map, but this would be overkill for this first-timer.

Together they could map out a small square foot garden of potatoes, garlic, chard, squash, and tomatoes. A few square feet would be dedicated to herbs that paired well in recipes with those plants— say, oregano, mint, and thyme. Easy plants with lots of recipes. If he really wanted to include or exclude particular items, he could let the agent know.

"Well I cannot stand mint. Tastes like toothpaste to me. But I do like coriander…" Swapping out a single item from a draft list would be easier than creating the list from scratch, especially to a first-time gardener.

A last bit here would be about getting the hardware. Mr. McGregor shows a starter kit for implements and lets Chuck remove any items he already has. Access to other accounts where it could check to see recent purchases might save him this work, too. Then Chuck could provide payment details and see that Mr. McGregor would keep an eye on the shipments for him. With the garden plan in place and the hardware en route, the agent has helped him set things in motion to have a garden and learn the tricks of the trade.

The Setup

When the hardware arrives, Chuck might need help setting it up. There's a solid argument to be made for connecting him with another user of Mr. McGregor's who lives near him, to get him into the community of practice and create an informal apprenticeship relationship, but let's see if we can solve it with just the product.

When Mr. McGregor detected that the hardware had arrived, it could send Chuck some short videos about installing the ground thermometers, the soil moisture sensors, and even the drip irrigation system. After he's installed them, it could walk him through testing it to make sure they're set up correctly. By being aware of events and preparing him for the next steps in advance, the agent could deliver information when it was most meaningful and actionable. Later, seeds and equipment would arrive, and Mr. McGregor could similarly supply some just-in-time information about how to plant the seeds and fertilize the ground.

The Bee is a special case. It needs to know where it should go to monitor the plants. Mr. McGregor could base a path on its map, or let Chuck specify this using GUI tools and the map of his backyard, but this might not take real things into account like lawn furniture or tall potted plants. Under "Getting Goals, Preferences, and Permissions > Implicitly," I discussed the agent's watching how a task was performed, and this is a good example. Mr. McGregor could explain to Chuck the goals of the demonstration (avoid wires, show the Bee each square foot in the garden, etc.) and have him carry the Bee from its charging station on a path that met those goals. The Bee could memorize the path as they walked. Mr. McGregor would need to run the Bee through the path once to make sure it could execute it correctly, but thereafter it could have the Bee use that same path as it went about its maintenance tasks, which we'll get to later.

Test Driving

A test drive doesn't make too much sense here. Of course the whole first year is a test for both Chuck and Mr. McGregor, but it's a *live* test. Fortunately, it's not too risky. At worst, Chuck will have lost some time and money with no homegrown crops to show for it. But he still has the grocery store. This section is included as an illustration that the breadth of agentive technology is great, and the patterns identified will not fit every application.

Launch

Once Chuck has the hardware and software up, the soil prepared, and the seeds sown, Mr. McGregor can let him know that much of the hard work is over with a celebration video and maybe even help him visualize that first tasty meal he'll be able to make from his garden in a few weeks or months. In an app, you could show live pictures of the garden with calm countdown timers as to the next activities, with reassurances that Mr. McGregor will reach out to him when the time comes. By thinking agentively, you could save Chuck the effort of having to track everything about the garden when he's first starting out.

CHAPTER 7

Everything Running Smoothly

Once an agent is up and running, it doesn't just disappear. It's not a light switch or an autofocus. In this chapter, we'll look at some scenarios that might happen while the agent is humming along.

As with the other scenarios described in this section, much of the final design will depend on the particulars of the agent and its domain.

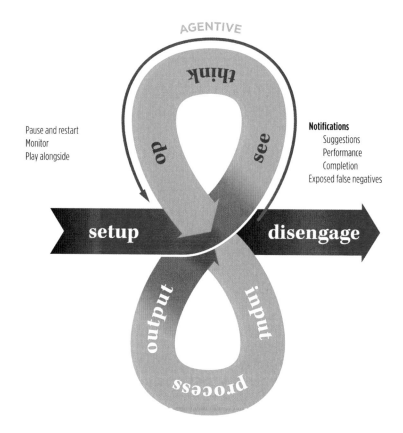

Pause and Restart

Some users will need the ability to pause and restart the agent. For example, the roboinvestor has to wait while its investor is laid off and looking for new regular income. The Roomba might need to be paused while its owner cleans up the cat puke before it gets algorithmically smeared all over the floor. Mr. McGregor offers a way to arrange a temporary gardener while Chuck is away on vacation. If the stakes of the system are high, these controls have to be very obvious and easily accessible. If the pause has a known end time, then you can even make the restart itself based on a trigger.

The paused mode has to be made very obvious. When the agent approaches a costly deadline or a trigger it would ordinarily respond to, this information should jump out at the user, since this is a possible missed opportunity. These missed-opportunity notifications shouldn't carry too much blame. As the layoff example illustrates, the pause may not be its fault.

Monitoring

Almost by definition, when the agent is doing its agentive thing, it will be out of sight. But it shouldn't cloak itself from a user who does want to check in. Is it still, you know, working? How do the accumulating results look, if there are any? How long until the next scheduled trigger? Are the data streams smooth and quiet, or wavy and trending? It may not be significant, since the agent would reach out if it had real concerns, but as long as the user is looking, show them what's happening.

Ambient displays and solid information graphics can convey a lot of this information in easily glanceable ways.

Let Me Play, Anyway

People are a vain lot. Even if the data suggest that they cannot beat the agent at its task, there will be some part of users that wonders if their human senses and experience can reveal something that the cold sensors and algorithms can't. Hunches happen for a reason. Who knows? In some cases, they may be right.

For these reasons, provide users with a way to play alongside the agent if they want. It might be with a virtual dataset or a small subset of the real resources.

If it's possible to compare the results of play against what the agent would have done with the same resources, overlaying this information provides an opportunity. If the agent performs better, it will let the user build trust in the agent. If the user performs better, it gives an opportunity to tune the agent. There might also be some important nuances to the way a user performs the task during play that can act as an implicit tuning. A driver might show her car how she prefers it to take tight corners, for example, and would rather demonstrate than try to describe it. She might also want to show how to take particular challenges. "You need to kind of build up a little speed to get over this weird bump and pothole combination in my friend's driveway. Watch me."

This car example reminds us that in some domains, users will *want* or *need* to maintain the skills necessary to do the task themselves, if for no other reason than to be able to handle the takeover scenario. The same functions by which a user might play with the task could be used in practice mode. See more about these considerations in the next two chapters.

Notifications

Agents almost by definition are out of sight as they do their agentive thing. But there are routine circumstances where the user needs to be tapped for input.

Completion

Hey, I'm done! Not every completed action deserves a ticker tape parade, but at the very least some sense of completion reminds the user that the system is working. Routine maintenance tasks might just warrant soft audio feedback or an entry in a log. If an agent overcame some challenges en route, that deserves some credit. Even if it was smooth sailing, this notification is an opportunity to remind the user of the value they receive from the agent and even the brand promise. My Roomba named Rusty has a bright and goofy little tune it plays when it makes it back to the charging station after a successful run and if I'm around to hear it, I'll admit it adds a little something.

Suggestions

One of the nifty promises of agents is that they can aid in the discovery of new opportunities. Chef Watson reaches out to me with recipes. Spotify shares a customized new music collection each week. Discovery is part of the brand promise for these services, but you can imagine other agents acting like helpful service professionals when they note some easy option that better suits your goals, helps you find a better route, or reminds you of something. Speaking of promises, if the promise of an agent is to do work on the user's behalf, suggestions run a grave risk of bothering the user and undermining the main point, so they need to be handled very gingerly, and only delivered where the confidence of value is very high.

Routine Contact/Performance

Being out of sight most of the time can result in an out-of-mind problem for the brand. What to do if the agent is still working fine, but it hasn't run into any triggers? Does it just fade away? If the user hasn't interacted with the agent for a while, it can reach out to confirm that it's still running. This reaching out runs the risk of being perceived as noisy marketing, so it should have respectful defaults and offer an opt-out or controls for frequency of such contact.

One of the things any user will be considering in the use of an agent is whether it is worth the hassle. I turned off AutoCorrect on my iPhone because I like to be creative with language, and the triple-correction bothered me: I type something, miss the tiny warnings it offers to indicate that it's about to correct me, have the actual correction be the thing that catches my eye, return to retype the text, and despite my having just corrected it once, have it autocorrect me again, forcing me to slow down, lose my flow, and retype the thing a *third* time watching for the warning to manually dismiss the correction. This has slowed me down and frustrated me frequently enough that I figured it just wasn't worth it. Similarly, Siri's transcription function is a great boon, as long as I'm talking about something short and mundane. But having to go back and parse a long transcription to correct it is much more mental effort than to just type it myself.

But my perception may be misinformed. What if, even with the triple corrections, I was *still* faster using AutoCorrect? Apple never gives me any information to counter my emotional perception of it. If by some reliable metric I could see that I was (or people like me were) faster with AutoCorrect, despite the babysitting it needs, I might have stuck with it. Understanding the value of an agent from an unemotional point of view is important. Even if the news is bad, and the agent is slowing down users, that's important for the provider to know, and virtuous for them to share that information with users, proactively.

Concern

Users should never be surprised by news unless the event that caused it was truly sudden. When any of the things of interest to the user begin to trend in a concerning way, that fact should be conveyed to the user in a meaningful and nonintrusive way. The notification should not be verbose, but should include the following information:

- A clear explanation.

- A mention of the threshold that's being approached.

- What the agent is doing about it.

- That the user will be contacted if the threshold is crossed.

- What the user ought to do in the meantime.

- What the user will be asked to do if the threshold is crossed.

...all in as friendly and concise language as possible, of course.

> Hey Carla. This message is to let you know that stocks in your Home Buying portfolio have been underperforming over the last few weeks. While it hasn't been significant enough to affect the portfolio's goals, if the trend continues over the next three weeks, it will be. If the stocks pick up (and we expect them to), there's nothing you'll need to do. If they continue to underperform, we'll contact you with some alternatives. If you'd like daily notifications about this portfolio's performance while we're keeping an eye on it, click here.

Problems

And, of course, the agent should reach out when things are trending poorly, or there are problems. These are important enough to warrant their own chapter, which comes next.

Recap: Smooth Sailing Is the Easy Part

When the agent is working, the user is getting maximum benefit for minimum input. It's not all set-and-forget, though. There are plenty of design questions to consider.

- **Pause and restart:** Give the users obvious controls to put the agent on hold and resume it again.

- **Monitoring:** Especially early in use, users may want to check in on the agent and see how it is performing. Provide a way for them to check on the agent, and help them understand and build confidence in the agent's performance.

- **Play:** Some users will want to play alongside the agent as it does its work, either to keep in practice, to handle a situation the agent didn't recognize, or to see if they can beat the agent at its own game. Facilitate the users so that they are doing this without interfering with the agent's work.

- **Notifications:** Even if the users are not pausing, monitoring, or playing alongside the agent, the agent may need to let them know some things. Design easy signals for the users to know if the agent is running, when it has completed tasks, and when it has concerns.

Running Smoothly

As mentioned in "Ramping Up," Chuck had a lot to do in setting up his vegetable garden, and you saw how agentive thinking helped make that awesome for Chuck. Once it's set up, though, there are some other agentive parts to consider. Let's move through some of the patterns for when he's doing the actual gardening.

Pause and Restart

It's true that living plants can't really be paused and restarted, but when we think about this pattern in relation to the problem, maybe Chuck's *gardening* can be. For example, if Mr. McGregor noticed that Chuck was in another city, it could ask if a temporary gardener should be arranged. It could find someone in Chuck's friend network, or if Potter partnered with a freelance-labor market like TaskRabbit, one could be hired, and Mr. McGregor could handle all the arrangements. (Noting that such "gig" platforms can have negative socio-economic effects.) All it would need to do is ask Chuck how long he'd be away (or permissions to the relevant data stream to avoid being surprised again) and confirm how much money he wants to spend. Chuck would get messages, tailored to his current time zone, to let him know when the temporary gardener had been arranged.

The zone-controlled drip irrigation is mostly automated. It takes information from the soil moisture sensors, compares that to ideal cycles of moisture for the plant at that location, and controls the irrigation accordingly. It's instructive to note that while this is a pause and restart of a component of the system, it's not of interest to Chuck unless something has gone wrong with it. This part of the system could largely be considered autonomous in regular use.

Monitoring During Growth

Growing season is when Mr. McGregor is at its most agentive—keeping an eye on the plants in the garden for problems, monitoring their soil, and watering them. During this period, Chuck will be kept informed, but he will only need to take action when there's a problem.

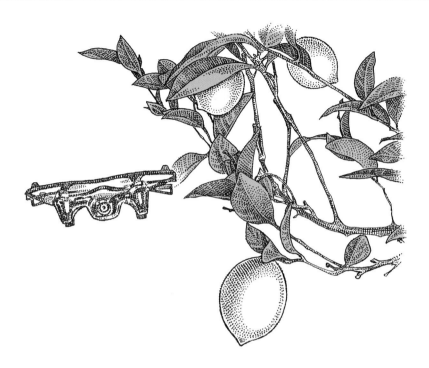

With the Bee trained, each day that weather permits, it can leave its charging perch to fly to the garden and capture multiple pictures of each plant before uploading them to servers for processing. Of course, Chuck would have access to the photos and to time-lapse videos of them. But Chuck isn't yet an enthusiast. He's unlikely to want that information daily when there's nothing really for him to do. He might like to see the time lapse of every inch of growth, though, and Mr. McGregor should send a test message after the first inch of growth is complete, so he can watch it stretch itself up out of the ground.

Moreover, the server should run image processing on the pictures to look for signs of disease, withering, or pests. If there appears to be no problem, the data is stored. No other action is necessary. We'll talk about problems it's confident it found later as exception handling. If its algorithm was unsure, it could pass information about the plant, the time-lapse images, and the question at hand to someone else in the network. That could be someone at Potter, if an expert were needed, or it could be another of the enthusiasts who use the service and have experience with gardening and that particular plant. Chuck doesn't have the expertise needed yet to recognize when his plants are in trouble, but agents should take advantage of the network they're a part of. Of course, if it turns out that his plants have a disease or pests that need taking care of, Mr. McGregor should walk Chuck through the remedy, including ordering supplies and helping him know what to do with them.

Play Anyway

Chuck doesn't just want to have the vegetables. He has a supermarket for that. He doesn't just want the garden either, as he could probably hire someone to come in and set transplants up for him if it came to that. He does want to *learn* how to garden, so he just wants the machines to do what they are good at, so it's less effort for him.

In the interest of learning, Mr. McGregor can reserve some portion of Chuck's garden—say one square foot at this early stage—for a plant that does not get monitored by the Bee and might be more finicky than the other starter plants. Chuck will get reminders to monitor and check this plant, and it's quite possible that Chuck will slip and not tend it. It might go to seed quickly or be eaten by snails. If he fails at it, he has an object lesson in doing better next time. At first, the agent might just hand him monitoring tasks. Once Chuck masters those, it could ease him into watering or fertilizing tasks. By stepping back a bit, the agent could help him begin to internalize the new skill of gardening without compromising the entire garden.

Something About the Reaping

Harvest time is when Chuck's patience begins to pay off, and it's also the beginning of more intensive labor, so it deserves a bit of fanfare. Mr. McGregor should give Chuck a few weeks' warning in a message so that he can make sure to set aside the time. It should set expectations on what he'll be doing and what to expect. It can also get him excited with some suggestions on what to do with the harvest—including time-lapse images of the growth to-date, and recipes for enjoying the vegetables fresh or storing them for later.

The messages during this time will come both on days off and workdays, so reminders should come at the right time, which can be inferred by Chuck's routine locations across the week. Harvest messages could include images taken by the Bee and run against image processors for helpful hints, like pointing out in an image exactly what the tomatoes should look like when ready for harvest and pointing out those that need a little more time on the vine.

Mr. McGregor could even prompt Chuck to take a selfie with his harvest that it could include along with the time-lapse images in a friendly brag post for social media.

Post-Harvest

Similar to soil preparation and sowing, Chuck will have some tasks after the harvest, like dealing with the withering vines of his tomato plants. These are important, but not useful for our purposes to get into details. For the sake of narrative, understand that yes, Mr. McGregor will help Chuck know about and accomplish those necessary tasks.

Suggestions and Learning

One of the things an agent can do is help its user discover things they might not have thought of. After Chuck's first successful year gardening with Mr. McGregor, it can contact him for a review of how things went. This information feeds into the agent's personalization for Chuck (no to mint, yes to coriander). Then a few weeks before the next planting season, the agent could contact Chuck with a plan for his garden in the upcoming year, including suggestions for new vegetables or herbs, expanding the garden, perhaps some trickier plants, and the opportunity for Chuck to take over more of the gardening from the agent. It might even have some suggestions on what to do to avoid problems encountered in last year's season.

CHAPTER 8

Handling Exceptions

One of my all-time favorite moments in school was when I was in 7th grade (around 12 years old for readers unfamiliar with American schooling structures). The homework assignment seemed simple at first: write instructions on how to make a peanut butter and jelly sandwich. It seemed suspiciously simple. When we came to class the next day, the teacher had set up a station with a loaf of bread, a jar of peanut butter, a jar of jelly, a bread knife, and a towel. A towel? What was that for? She then collected the assignments and picked one of them, announcing to the class that she would be following these instructions like a computer might.

She read the first step of the first assignment aloud, "Put peanut butter on the first slice of bread." To our collective shock and laughter, she took the unopened jar of peanut butter and placed it on one end of the still-bagged loaf of bread. She then moved on to the next instruction. Over the course of a few of these first-draft assignments, she acted as a "strict interpreter" (or, OK, a malicious interpreter) to our instructions and wound up doing all sorts of crazy things, like smearing jelly on the bread bag, making sandwiches with the condiments on the outside, and smearing peanut butter with her hands instead of with knives. (It became clear why she needed the towel.)

Halfway through the class, she explained that the way she was acting was the way a computer understands the instructions you give it—very literally, and that it could not infer missing information like a human could. She gave us about 15 minutes to write a new instruction/program that might result in an edible PB&J. I tore into this problem, eager to outthink this troublesome "computer." I don't think she got to my program that class, but I never forgot the lesson. Computers don't think like humans do, and so are prone to what we would call errors, but what the computer would just call following instructions it was given.

Until we get to general artificial intelligence, this will continue to be true. Try as we may, the agentive technology we create will not be perfect. Since we humans have a general intelligence and by definition agents don't, they're going to miss some things we would think of, or run into situations they can't handle. Given that they're going to fail at some point, we want to design them so that they fail well. To do this, we'll look at tuning triggers and behaviors, trend alerts, alarms, and handoff scenarios.

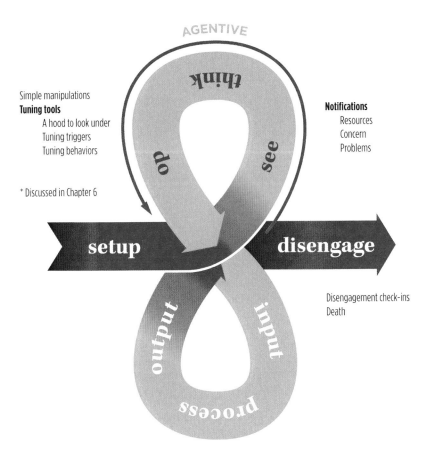

AGENTIVE

think

Simple manipulations
Tuning tools
   A hood to look under
   Tuning triggers
   Tuning behaviors

* Discussed in Chapter 6

op

see

Notifications
Resources
Concern
Problems

setup

disengage

Disengagement check-ins
Death

output

input

process

Where Do These Interfaces Go?

On agents with physical components, the interfaces for these tasks
may be the object itself. Correcting a Roomba, for example, can
involve simply putting your foot in front of it to stop its forward
progress. Interfaces could also be on the object: think physical
controls and 7-segment displays, touch screens, or microphones
and speakers for voice interactions. But these interfaces don't need
to reside on the object. More and more, designers are shifting the
burden of display and control to the cloud and letting users use their
desktop computers or smartphones as the interface. This reduces
the cost of the hardware by eliminating displays and controls, and it
replaces them with app development, unique IDs, and cloud communication components. Those systems need to consider security
features and authentication flows as part of your designs.

A Nod to the Looping, Careening Rollercoaster of Trust

I am presenting use cases throughout this section simply and linearly for the sake of explanation, but in practice, dealing with trust and failure is a messier affair.

For starters, the amount of trust you afford any agent depends on the tasks you ask it to perform on your behalf. When the risk of failure is small, such as an unswept floor, you can afford it a great deal of agency from the get-go. When the risk is great, such as your physical well-being or financial solvency, it may take many years before you're willing to feel trust and grant them full agency to act on your behalf.

It's made more complicated by these issues:

- **The complexity of tasks.** Tasks are often made up of many smaller subtasks. Each of the subtasks can be automatic, assistive, or agentive. The failure of one can lower the trust of the whole thing.

- **The layers of scope.** Agents may be trusted to start with small tasks and only after demonstrating a competence in those is a user willing to let it help with larger tasks or ultimate goals.

- **The reputation of the providing organization.** One or two public missteps in the handling of privacy, or of putting the business goals at too great a cost to the user, and the user's distrust of the brand will spill over to the agents it provides.

Regardless of where that level of trust starts, over dozens or even hundreds of interactions, every time the system succeeds, the user will grant it more trust and leeway. Every time the system fails and you have to help get it back on track, you will have to rebuild trust that the new settings (and any new algorithms) are correct. It's an unfair rollercoaster because trust is built slowly over many interactions, and it can all fall quickly with a few failures. Or even one bad one.

All of this underscores the notion that because agentive technology operates mostly out of sight, trust becomes a major issue in the design of these systems. How you handle the exceptions and handoffs is the bulk of your work, because it is so critical.

Limited Resources

Batteries and hard drive space, bandwidth, and the 150-close-friend limit—few systems work without some sort of limited resource, even if it's imposed by a subscription-levels scheme. Agents should keep an eye on these resources and notify their users when the resource is running low or needs management. You must ensure that the notification comes in time for users to do something about it.

The Prospero robo-farmer is an agentive planting drone that works in swarms to plant seeds in fields very quickly, even on tricky terrain. If the Prospero robots are running low on seeds to plant, the (human) farmer may need an hour's notification to leave the field to meet up with them at the barn for refills. Automated backup drives may want to let users know they're getting full, weeks in advance, to schedule some in-depth time to curate files, pause the backup, or purchase more space.

Simple Manipulations

In some cases, robots run by agents will simply run into physical problems. The Roomba gets stuck under the overhang of your cabinetry. An agentive pet feeder's bin is jammed with kibble. The autohelm's handle was knocked by a drunken passenger. Providing the users are alerted to the problem, the agent should be able to handle a simple physical correction by the user without going haywire.

The Roomba's algorithm doesn't depend on being set down in the same spot. The auger can just continue spinning when the kibble jam is cleared. The handle can just be put back in place. People are imprecise, and agents can't expect precision from them as they help the agent correct these physical problems.

• • •

When the agent runs into trouble executing its instructions, users need ways to save the individual case as well as improve instructions for the future. This can come in the form of tuning its instructions—either the triggers it looks for to take actions, or the actions themselves. See more on each in the following sections.

Tuning Triggers

As agents monitor data streams to do their job, they are deciding when variables meet their trigger conditions and when they don't. Simple events like a time-of-day are unlikely to run into problems, but more sophisticated triggers will run into problems of false positives and false negatives.

Refine False Positives

When the agent believes its trigger conditions have been met, but it's not what the human intended, it counts as a *false positive*. Some examples to illustrate: Spotify plays a song that the listener doesn't like. ShotSpotter sends officers to investigate a backfiring car. Volvo's smart truck brakes before a steaming manhole.

In these cases, the users will almost certainly notice the error and want to resolve it. They can either skip the current case or seek to tune the trigger conditions.

Skip This Case for Now

When the cost of the false positive is low—as with a song that is merely not to the listener's liking—you can provide a simple mechanism to skip the current case. For example, it's possible that I'm not in a Russian Polka Metal mood right now, but might be later, so I am OK just skipping it for now. Other examples include kicking the Roomba out of the kitchen while a complicated meal is underway, or telling ShotSpotter to ignore the neighborhood skeet shooting competition. This last example shows that the skip may need some additional detail, like a duration or location to ignore.

Skip now is a temporary exception. Anytime the user adds a permanent exception or rule, it can be thought of as *tuning* the triggers. But the agent—in true agentive fashion—doesn't need to wait for the user to do the tuning. Clever agents should keep track of things that are skipped and see if they can infer the reasons for skipping with high confidence. If that's the case, the agent can float the new rule for approval the next time a case is skipped, or if the cost is low, just build it into the trigger algorithm without asking.

> Hi, Karen. I notice this is the third time you've asked me to divest your portfolio of a tobacco stock. Would you like me to just avoid them altogether in the future?

Changing the Trigger

What an agent *responds to* is, conceptually, half of what makes it up. (The other half is its *behavior*, as covered in "Tuning Behaviors.") When triggers are wrong, the whole value of the agent is in question, so it's important to get them right, and if it makes sense for users to adjust them, to make those tuning interfaces right.

Request Review

Consider Volvo's self-braking truck. It identifies moving objects and predicts their trajectories. If it predicts any are on a collision course, and the driver hasn't applied the brakes quickly enough, the agent applies them instead. It's unreasonable to expect that the driver would want or know how to tune the agent on the road before restarting the truck and continuing on her way. But expecting her to remember to do it later is also unreasonable. In these cases, it's best to allow her to indicate that a problem happened, automatically capture as much of the *in situ* data as possible, and allow her to add any additional comments. Then the next time it's on a network it can send this data back to Volvo, which will use it to refine the algorithms on all their trucks.

An example of this kind of feedback appears on mobile versions of Google Maps, which has a feature called, plainly, "Shake to send feedback." When turned on, after a user shakes her phone (presumably in frustration), the app captures a screenshot of the app in use and offers to send it along with any additional feedback to the developers.

The tools for tuning triggers will depend greatly on the domain, but for the remainder of this section, I'll stick with the example of a music agent akin to Pandora or Spotify, as the data objects are rich and the interactions are familiar to most people.

Add to a Blacklist

If my favorite Russian Polka Metal band recorded that one crooning country love ballad that I just can't stand, and it gets slipped into my music stream, then I need to tell my music agent that I want this specific case to be an exception to the general rule about Russian Polka Metal. An "ignore forever" option lets me quickly establish the exception without getting into more complicated rule management. Users need options to review and manage this list, or at the very least to eliminate it to start over. If users grant permission, blacklists can be shared back with the developer as additional information to feed into refining the artificial intelligence's general understanding of the domain.

But these easy options won't make sense for every agentive domain.

Most of the time the agent should be able to accept the exception without fanfare and move on. However, if the additional exception has a significant impact on the future performance of the agent, it may need to speak up and let the user know, unobtrusively, so the user can manage the problem.

Add or Modify a Rule

Sometimes the user will want to ensure that nothing like the false positive happens again. To do that they'll need to create or modify a general rule. If the risks are low and the inference algorithm is confident, it can happen automatically. If the costs are high or the confidence low, let the user verify a suggested change, as in the tobacco stock example cited previously. But, if the costs are high or manual control is needed, you'll have to help users manually manage the rules that govern the trigger. This is not an easy task because on the surface rules can seem simple, but they can get complex quickly.

Simple: Don't play country music.

Middling: Play country music recorded before 1979.

Complex: Play music that is classified as either country or western and recorded before 1979, or if it was recorded between 1980 and 2000 and either subclassified as "alternative country" or a Billboard top-10 hit.

Readers familiar with the database language SQL will recognize it as a logical set of predicates that needs an explicit parsing order. Readers unfamiliar with SQL language can infer that humans and their preferences can be quite specific, and getting those preferences into a structure that the computer can understand is itself tricky and complicated. I've designed around a dozen of similar controls over my career, building on patterns shared with me by thought partners at former employers, and what follows is an abstracted solution called a *constrained natural language builder.* This is just one way to tackle the problem, of course, but one that has evolved in use across several disparate domains and several design pairs I've been in, and is based on the fundamentals of human psychology and language.

Constrained Natural Language Builder

Let users adjust the rule from within the context of the false positive, so you can highlight the reasons the case was considered correct. Then users can focus on refining those things.

You should provide a plain language statement of the trigger. Then highlight the elements that can be adjusted. Allow controls to delete existing clauses and provide a clear tool for adding a new clause. When the user opts to modify a parameter or operators, show available options so she doesn't have to commit them to memory. (Ideally, this activity happens rarely, so you don't want to presume any expertise.) Try to keep the operators in plain language. When the user adjusts a variable, provide a tool that makes it easy to enter and makes it difficult to make errors.

Adjacent to these controls, it's important to show a preview of what would happen if the new rule were run. This can't just be a random sample of results, as it might not show the edge cases that make or break the rule. For example, if for a music agent I'd manually set the complex example, you could show me a list of all music that would be included in the new results, but since country makes up a small percentage of songs that I like, that list might not show a single country song at all. That doesn't help me know whether the new rule is satisfying my request. It's better to show lists made up of the following:

- The cases that match the new trigger, but previously made it through without objection.

- The cases that *match* the new trigger, but only just barely.

- The cases that *fail* the new trigger, but only just barely.

This lets your user continue tweaking the rule until the boundary looks satisfying in both its definition and its expected effects. If you have screen real estate, you can also show a general sampling of results rather than just edge cases, but it will be of secondary importance.

Of course, music agents aren't really costly enough to warrant this kind of minute refining, but it's an accessible example for explaining the issues, in lieu of more critical but harder to explain financial, medical, or safety agents.

These are the basics of the constrained natural language builder. We'll return to it later in the chapter to discuss modifying behavioral rules.

A quick note on channel: until we get to perfect language comprehension and expression, I strongly suspect that modifying rules through audio or language will be cumbersome. It can work if the possible rules are simple and easily guessable by your users, but powerful or comprehensive rules will benefit from the nonlinear nature of visual presentation.

Expose False Negatives

When the agent skips over something that the user would have expected to trigger, it counts as a *false negative*. Looking at the earlier examples again: Spotify misses a song that the listener would have just loved to hear. ShotSpotter ignores actual shots fired. Volvo's smart truck barrels into a child's bouncing ball.

For some false negatives, the user will certainly notice. This is true with agents that help you avoid something, like Volvo's self-braking truck. The driver will forcefully apply the brake after she hits the ball, to make sure it's not followed by a child chasing it. She'll then wonder what's going on with the brake agent and want to make sure it learns to stop for bouncing balls.

But *most* false negatives will go unnoticed. That one song will go unloved. The criminal shooters get away if no one reports the sound.

So the main challenge is to occasionally expose cases that were just barely rejected, in order to make sure that the settings are still correct. I suspect that spam filters work this way, letting one through every now and then, even if it's confident that it's spam. This reminds the user that the spam agent is still there, still working on their behalf, but also prompts them to go check into recent rejects to double-check. It is in the context of this rejects list that the user can declare one case to be an exception via a whitelist.

Like false positives, users should be able to explicitly declare that an item should be included. "Even though it qualifies for rejection, I want you to trigger on *this*." There doesn't need to be a reason, but to help the agent get smarter, give the user the chance to share *why* it gets an exception with the agent. (Is it the recording artist? The genre? The beats-per-minute?) Clever agents in low-risk domains can infer the reasons why it was listed and update rules implicitly. Agents in more critical domains can ask users to vet inferred rules or provide access to tools for adding/modifying a rule. If users grant permission, whitelists and the rules they "break" can be shared back with the developer as additional information to feed into refining the artificial intelligence.

Add or Modify a Rule

Keep a list of rejects available to the user so she can double-check the results. Let the list be complete, but offer a quick filter to review just the edge cases where the agent's confidence was low. Otherwise, this should work just like the rule management described earlier, under "Refine False Positives."

Tuning Behaviors

Triggers tell an agent when to *act*. Behaviors tell an agent what to *do*, by describing goals and methods to achieve those goals. Since they are the other "half" of the agent, when the behaviors are wrong, the value of the agent is in question, so these interfaces need to be usable and effective.

Some agents will have fixed behaviors that can't really be modified. The Roomba (at the time of writing anyway) doesn't learn your home's floor plan or where the carpet is most often messy. It obeys an algorithm that was developed by iRobot corporation specifically to maximize coverage of any floor plan you might throw at it. You can certainly pick it up and put it down in a place you want it to focus on for a while, but this is an aspect of "play" (see Chapter 7, "Everything Running Smoothly"). To tune a behavior is to change the goal or refine its methods.

Tuning Goals

Goals are the values that the agent will try to meet within a span of time. There are certainly higher-order goals, like "keeping comfortable," but the Nest Thermostat needs to resolve that to actual temperatures and humidities, calendars, and geolocations. The autohelm needs to know a bearing or its destinations and the time by which it should try to get to each.

Many simple agents have their goals built in. My Roomba will always just sweep the floor. My Get Narrative will always just help me life blog. The pest-agent Orbit Yard Enforcer will only ever turn its sprinkler on to frighten animals that set off its motion sensor. But for more sophisticated or complex agents, goals may be changed in advance of behaviors or even midcourse.

The design of tools to tune goals will depend on their domain. An autohelm may have you turning a dial to indicate a bearing, while the auto-acquisitions library agent needs a full WIMP interface. As tools for users, these interfaces will be informed by the patterns and best practices the HCI/IxD/UX community has developed over its existence. It's beyond the scope of this book to recount those patterns, but the good news is there are decades of resources available to learn more.

Tuning Methods

Methods are the different ways the agent can pursue users' goals. It includes any constraints the user sets. The intelligent portfolio can help the investor achieve her retirement goals aggressively with high risk, or conservatively with low risk, but it can't make that determination on her behalf. She can tell it to avoid any "vice stocks" like alcohol, gambling, and tobacco, or alternatively to focus heavily on these recession-proof instruments. These are examples of methods.

The tools you provide for users to tune methods can be both physical and virtual. If the agent inhabits a bot or exists in physical space, then physical steps can be taken to tune the behavior. While physical controls can be adopted for digital agents, most often they will be tuned virtually.

Physical: Do It Like This

If you had to move your Roomba to the same spot a handful of times, it should take the hint to make sure and hit that spot in future cleanings. (But it doesn't yet.) That would be a positive and implied tuning, as in "Here's what I want you to do." If you dropped a couple of "virtual wall" beacons onto the floor, forbidding it from venturing too near the oven, you're tuning it negatively, by establishing its constraints physically. With a Tesla car, returning to the hairpin curve and telling it to watch how you handle it, is a physical demonstration. Push the Prospero robot a little deeper into the dirt and say, "Also, tell the others they need to plant the seed this deep for it to take root" is another physical demonstration that also illustrates how one agent can share its information with its peers. This physical demonstration works well when the agent is embodied in some object, and the user has some expertise that is easy to demonstrate.

Virtual: Let Me Tell You

Physical interfaces won't make sense for every agent. For these, the interfaces to understand, add, and modify methods must be virtual. This could be a spoken conversation, or a chatbot, or a WIMP interface. Like tools for tuning goals, the exact manifestation is a question for interaction design. So, although the patterns selected for a particular agent will depend on its particulars, there are some use cases to consider.

A Menu of Options

If there are common methods, these can be presented as simple modes to pick from. The Furuno NavPilot 711C is an autohelm.[1] With its sonar, a captain can identify a fish or an underwater feature, and turn on one of five "FishHunter" modes, which pilot the boat in patterns in relation to the target: spiral, figure 8, square, zig zag, and orbit. The captain need only select one of these modes, and the agent takes it from there. A menu of options removes the burden of having to provide detailed instructions, offering up common or likely methods. The designer's challenge will be to research and provide the right options.

---

1 http://www.furunousa.com/ProductDocuments/NAVpilot711C%20
   Operator's%20Manual%20ver%20F.pdf

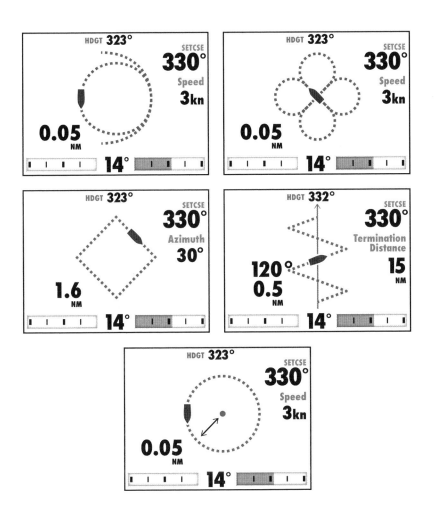

Sharing an Example: Do It Like That

If the user doesn't have the expertise but can point to an example that the agent can parse, then it reduces the amount of work to simply say, *like that*. Of course, you should be able to tell your new Nest Thermostat to handle things exactly like the old, broken one, but it also might mean going to set up your grandparent's Nest and being able to tell it, "start like our old house in Fresno." This relies on having access to that data, which privacy concerns may prevent.

Modifying Linguistic Rules

If individual use is too idiosyncratic for simple options, or if users would benefit from a "power" option in addition to simple options, you could provide access to constrained natural language descriptions for the methods using tools similar to what were illustrated earlier.

- ...keep the temperature within 15°C and 30°C.

- ...keep patch 14 the ideal moisture for radishes.

- ...apply the label "likely spam," and move the message to the trash.

Rather than asking users to build these from scratch, the system can begin with smart defaults, which can then be modified.

Note that the triggers and methods should be shown together, since it is the combination of both that makes up the rule.

- **When the home is empty,** keep the temperature within 15°C and 30°C.

- **When the season is spring,** keep patch 14 the ideal moisture for radishes.

- **When an email is received and it contains the phrase "Canadian Pharmacy" and is not from someone in my contacts list,** apply the label "likely spam," and move the message to the trash.

I imagine that in the future, users may want to share or sell well-structured rule sets for complex agents. This might even mean submitting rules to a marketplace where rule sets are reviewed and modified. Imagine being able to select a "Department of Energy" rule set for Nest.

Handoff and Takeback

When, despite all anticipatory efforts, an agent runs into a situation it simply cannot handle, the agent may need to ask the user not to modify the rule so that it can continue, but rather to ask the user to take back control. This action is called *handoff,* and when the user passes control back to the agent, it's called *takeback.* Note that this is distinct from *play,* which is more about the user wanting to use the agent's tools while the agent continues to do its work. Handoff and takeback are major issues, so they warrant their own chapter (see Chapter 9, unsurprisingly called "Handoff and Takeback").

Not all agents need to consider a handoff scenario. If the Nest Thermostat ever encounters a situation it's unable to cope with, the user has bigger problems than what to do about the thermostat. Similarly, if Spotify isn't working, it's more likely a problem with the network than with the agent's inability to pick a next song. And in low-stakes agentive tech, it may just not matter that the agent, say, skipped that unintelligible song. Who cares?

Disengagement and Death

Of course, agentive technology should allow users to opt out gracefully with no explanation, if that's how they want to handle it. Holding users hostage is rude, and it's bad business. Design attention should be paid to making the disengagement painless, if not polite and delightful. A natural place for this opt-out control is within notifications that come from the agent. But some agents, like eBay's persistent search, may just run out of things to notify a user about. *"Hey,"* it might say, *"No one has posted a Betamax copy of* The Garbage Pail Kids Movie *in a couple of years. Would you like to close this persistent search?"*

Death is another and quite sensitive topic. For some agents, identifying and correcting users who have passed away won't matter; they can keep finding shirts in the right size and sending them to the inactive email address. It's just noise in someone else's system. But with others, like Betterment's roboinvestor, if it can detect that its user has passed, it needs to find a next of kin and shift from asset planning and investing to transferring the estate.

Recap: Handling Exceptions Is Often the Hard Part

It's tempting to want to think of exceptions as rare and thereby consider them secondary. But exception cases are of primary importance because that's where the users will need to be the most engaged with the agent. If the agent doesn't degrade gracefully, it could cause more trouble than it's ultimately worth, and cause users to stop using them. It's fine for users to decide they no longer need a particular agent, but it would be unfortunate if it were really about the design rather than the utility.

- **Limited resources:** Signal when the agent is running out of something that it needs to run and how the user can replenish it most easily.

- **Simple manipulations:** If the agent is embodied in a robot, ensure that the user can make corrections physically. Ensure that the agent can seamlessly resume its work afterward.

- **Tuning triggers:** Design easy controls to correct the agent when it reacts to things it shouldn't.

- **Tuning behaviors:** Design easy controls to correct the agent when it behaves in undesirable ways.

- **Disengagement and death:** Ensure that the agent can detect whether it has outlived its use or its user and gracefully handle the disengagement. Pass control to another if appropriate. If it is difficult to detect these, provide for a hibernation mode.

Handling Exceptions

In "Running Smoothly" (see Chapter 7), we looked at how thinking agentively helped us envision the routine parts of the experience for Chuck. In this sidebar, we'll look at how it might help with the troublesome parts. To learn more about these patterns generally, read Chapters 8 and 9, "Handling Exceptions" and "Handoff and Takeback."

Just Blech

This season, Chuck took Mr. McGregor's suggestions and tried to grow some kale. He's tried some bites of leaves from the plant itself and is dubious, but willing to give it a try with the first recipe that's been suggested for kale fritters. Mr. McGregor notifies him of the harvest day, and Chuck gathers it, cleans it, and follows the recipe. He sets the table, serves himself the fritters, cuts off a bit with his fork, and pops it in his mouth. He finds it revolting. He wonders if he did something wrong, and decides to stick it out for the next recipe, kale and bean soup. But, no, that fails his taste test as well, and Chuck decides that kale is not for him. He grabs his phone and tells his app that the kale just isn't working out.

Mr. McGregor says there are a few things he can do, either composting the kale, donating it to a local food shelter, or offering it to the McGregor network to see if anyone would like to trade it for something from their garden. Whatever he decides, Mr. McGregor will help him arrange it, and it also modifies the rule for his profile. The system would certainly note a strong distaste for kale, but might also note to keep an eye out for other bitter veggies, and if he doesn't like a few of them, change the rule to note that bitterness isn't his thing.

Bzzz bzzz bzz, I'm Stuck

As Chuck approaches home one day, he sees a message that the Bee was unable to complete its rounds and got stuck. The message includes a photo it took right before it went into sleep mode, but it's mostly dark, so that doesn't help. Mr. McGregor notes that the Bee is now in the backyard, and lets Chuck know that he's going to have the Bee pulse its rotors to help Chuck locate it. When it starts to pulse, Chuck can quickly tell that it's located among the bushes. He follows the sound and when he finds it, he tells Mr. McGregor to stop the pulses so he can safely grab it and put it back on its charging base. Mr. McGregor then suggests he handle the day's inspections and tells him what to look for.

More Data

One day, the Bee's image processors notice some ants crawling on one of Chuck's plants, and it strongly indicates there may be aphids setting up camp under the leaves. Despite its maneuverings, the Bee can't get a good view of the underside of the leaves. So it takes a few extra pictures to include in a message to Chuck when he gets home about the possible problem and what he needs to do to correct it. Chuck turns it up and sees something, but isn't quite sure what it might be. He takes a picture and shares it. This message gets routed to the network, similar to how it did in the "Monitoring During Growth" scenario, which reports back that yes, he has aphids. Mr. McGregor intercepts the message and includes some easy remedies that Chuck could try before he turns to pesticides.

Mr. Snow Miser

Austin freezes maybe once every year. It's a rare occasion, but one which gardeners need to watch out for. Fortunately, because Mr. McGregor has access to the almanac and weather data, it can alert Chuck in advance and help him avoid problems. Even if Chuck has some cold-hearty plants in the ground, if it stays below −3.9°C for two hours, it should warn him that they're going to suffer major damage unless he puts on a coat, heads out there, and drops a blanket or a row cover on them. Fortunately, Chuck had the row cover on hand because Mr. McGregor saw that a cold snap was coming, and after making sure that it fit into the monthly budget, ordered it automatically.

Local Fauna

One day the Bee notices from its charging perch some unusual motion in the garden and sends some video to Chuck at work. Chuck sees that it's a deer with its muzzle in the carrots, and confirms that yes, he'd like the Bee to scare it away. He's connected to live video showing the Bee starting up its rotors and heading toward the deer, which bolts at the angry-wasp sound almost immediately. The Bee returns to its charging station and shuts down the live video. Chuck confirms that he wants the Bee to do this every time it detects an animal in the garden. Such are the costs of living near a park.

• • •

Each of these problems illustrates how the agent monitors its data streams and acts according to its goals and constraints to help Chuck. It even enlists his help when it runs into problems it can't handle to solve them collaboratively.

CHAPTER 9

Handoff and Takeback

As mentioned in Chapter 4, "Six Takeaways from the History of Agentive Thinking," automation and agentive thinking were originally developed when computer resources were scarce and the systems critical. Mountains of money could be at stake on a factory floor. A plane could fall out of the sky and kill everyone aboard. Soldiers and battles could be lost.

In that chapter, I noted that many early thoughts about automation and agents presumed that computers would become replacements for human actors in these systems, with humans acting as fail-safes—picking up where the agent failed. This made sense because computers are fast and precise, infinitely patient and attentive even in routine.

But over time, it became clear that simple replacement is not at all what happens. Having a computer do some of the work changes the nature of the system. Part of this is because computers miss some key human capabilities like pattern recognition, inductive reasoning, judgment, and nearly effortless access to relevant long-term memories. Additionally, computers are limited to their ontologies, their models of the world, and they can't detect changes to context or change outside of those models, and so have troubles adapting to it. Humans have to attend pretty constantly to correct those models and keep computers stable against the world's actual chaos.

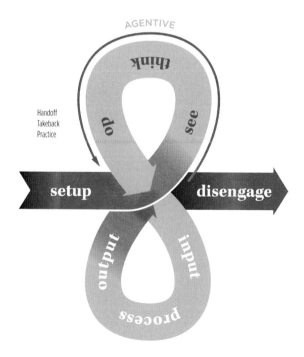

My favorite metaphor for all of this is Don Norman's, who noted that asking for help from a 5-year-old to do the dishes is not *just* getting help. You also must keep an eye on the 5-year-old's safety, progress, and understanding throughout. If it's not clear, narrow AI is that 5-year-old doing the dishes.

Does This Mean No AI?

But more than these problems of capability, one of the great ironies of automation in the past was that the people who were put in charge of taking over a process for a failing agent had become less and less equipped to do so, because of the presence of the agent. They no longer maintained a "big picture" of the whole system in their heads, which was needed to diagnose a problem and seamlessly enact corrections. Arguably worse, they were out of practice in performing the task, and so little better than newbies when trying to remedy the situation.[1]

These challenges and risks were so great that interaction design visionary Don Norman asserted that if there couldn't be full, completely reliable automation there should be no automation at all. Rather, designers should craft assistive technologies where computers and humans cocreate continuously and cooperatively.[2]

All of that said, it's important to note that Bainbridge and Norman are often writing in the context of critical systems, where lives and profits can be at stake. But what if the costs of system failure are not downed airplanes, but rather unclean floorboards? Or the handoff and takeback not as costly, as with changing the temperature in the home? Or you are designing consumer agents where co-creation is neither possible nor desirable because of human bias, as in a robo-investor? Or even where great expertise to correct problems is just not necessary? For these less critical systems, handoff and takeback may be manageable, and there are important considerations for passing awareness and control back and forth between the agent and the user.

---

1 Bainbridge, L. Brief paper: Ironies of automation. *Automatica* (Journal of IFAC). (archive) Vol. 19, Iss. 6, November, 1983, 775-779.

2 Keynote talk presented at the Automated Vehicles Symposium, San Francisco Airport, 2014, transcript available at www.jnd.org/dn.mss/the_human_side_of_au.html.

Just 30 Minutes of Vigilance

People are terrible at vigilance. Back in the 1940s, a researcher named Norman Mackworth made formal studies about how long people could visually monitor a system for "critical signals." He made a "clock" with a single ticking second hand that would jump every second, but which would irregularly jump forward two seconds instead of one. He would then sit his unfortunate test subjects in front of it for *two hours* and ask them to press a button when the clock jumped. Then he tracked each subject's accuracy over time. It turns out that, in general, people could go for around half an hour before their vigilance would significantly decay, and they would begin missing jumps. This loss of attention has little consequence in a testing environment, but Mackworth was studying the vigilance limits of WWI radar operators, when missing a critical signal could mean life or death.

> **NOTE BONE UP NOW**
>
> If you want to prepare for the off-chance that you'll find yourself facing one of these boredom devices but still want to do well, search for Brian Shackel's article "How I Broke the Mackworth Clock Test," as he shares his technique there.

You might think the solution is for users to monitor critical systems so they can take over quickly, but as noted previously, people are terrible at vigilance. After 30 minutes, their ability to monitor the system degrades sharply. So monitoring might work for short bursts, but it also turns out that it's not the only challenge in managing the handoff.

Decreasing Expertise

One of the consequences of handing tasks off to computers is that humans become worse at the tasks and less able to handle the emergency situations that the computer cannot handle. This is partly due to atrophying cognitive and physical skills associated with practice, as well as increasing difficulty in building a system-level awareness that would inform a diagnosis of the problem and constrain the solution. In Bainbridge's studies, this inability to handle exceptions was noticeable in the first generation of task-doers, who had built an expertise manually before becoming task managers. The effect was significantly greater in subsequent generations who had never built up expertise in the first place.

Some systems, like the Google driverless car, will be built presuming total agent control and consequently the loss of expertise by users. Other systems, like the Tesla driverless car, presume some level of vigilance and expertise. How can we design for a level of expertise that stands to decline with disuse?

Handing Off to Intermediates

So, to design the handoff from an agent to a person, you can't count on vigilance, and it's questionable whether you can count on the expertise of the user. Practice may help (see "Actual Practice" that follows), but may be too tedious for consumer applications. One way around the expertise problem is to hand the problem not to the user, but to a remote operator. In the case of self-driving cars, imagine an office in New Mexico somewhere, full of what looks like driving simulators. "Telechauffers" occupy these seats. These workers are trained specifically to take control of cars whose narrow AI is about to fail. Riders in the car hear a *thunk* as the LIDAR (Light Detection and Ranging) is knocked off the roof, and a screen illuminates with a video of a telechauffer saying, *"Hello, (reading from her screen) Mr. Noessel, I'm Helen. There's no need for alarm. While there is a problem with your car's sensors, control has already been passed to me, and I'll be completing the rest of the trip manually for you."*

Another option is to hand off control to any active agents in the same area. One car's LIDAR may be knocked off, but in heavy traffic, there may be eight cars around it that are still operational. The car may be blind, but the herd can help. The car should be able to announce its need for assistance and have cars around it (and buildings, and roads, and street lamps...) instantly share their sensor information in real time to help complete the compromised ride safely.

These intermediary strategies won't work for every agentive system, but should be considered as options.

Handing Off to the User

Years ago I had the opportunity to take a "Tiger Cruise" with a friend of mine who was an officer in the Navy, which is when a vessel travels from friendly port to friendly port and sailors can invite civilian friends or family to join and experience life at sea. During the week-long cruise, we watched many drills as the crew rehearsed again and again how they would manage the ship when various systems broke down. How they would use the voice tubes if the electronic communications failed. How they would line up and shout instructions from person to person if the voice tubes failed. How they would get teams to manually push the rudder if the ship's wheel no longer worked. These rehearsals kept the crew's skills fresh and in muscle memory.

This kind of practice may seem tedious from the individual's perspective, but is vital for the graceful degradation of this high-risk system. In a real emergency, no one had to look at a manual to remember the protocols. They'd likely just done it in the prior month.

Actual Practice

The Tiger Cruise example points to one way that users can prepare for takeover tasks—rote practice—just doing it often enough that skills stay fresh. Agents don't need to disappear completely during these moments, but they may take more of a backseat or feedback role. Routine practice can happen on a set schedule so that users expect and can plan on the takeover. "No, Thursday's commute won't work for the call. That's my driving practice morning. How about Friday?"

That said, practice should include both routine operation and emergency takeover situations as well. People have fire drills in buildings to ensure that they are not trying to figure out *how* to escape the burning building when they should just be escaping the burning building, and handling critical takeover is similar. Some emergency takeover should happen specifically when the user is engaged in something else, since part of the skill of takeover is ceasing the prior task.

Additionally, practice should ideally cover a broad range of conditions. So if a car learns that it will soon encounter icy conditions that are rare for the driver, it can take advantage of the opportunity to share that knowledge and offer the practice opportunity.

Some takeover practice will need to feel like a real emergency, which, in turn, implies that real emergencies may need, as cliché as it may seem, to specify when "this is not a drill."

High-Fidelity Virtual Practice

If actual practice is, well, impractical, it may be possible to provide high-fidelity virtual practice. This isn't as desirable because few simulations are so high-fidelity that they play out perfectly in the real world, but then again, doctors won't always have a patient on hand with the right malady, and storms won't adhere to a schedule so that pilots can practice flying in them. So a virtual replacement or simulator is a fine stand-in for these cases, and the goal will be to make it as realistic as possible. If this is the route your agent takes, look into the work of Ivan Sutherland's 1967 Scanned Beetle or Ted Nelson's writings about simulation at PARC.

Interface Considerations

The notifications mentioned in Chapter 7, "Everything Running Smoothly," worked whether they were asynchronous or not. But in a handoff situation, you're squarely in the land of interface tasks, so these recommendations are more strongly made about the UI.

Trending Monitors

Users of critical systems need to be kept abreast of agentive tasks, and not just when things are dire. Norman contrasts an autopilot that hums along until it panics—and only then does the pilot learn there was a problem at all—with an autopilot that reports its troubles in stages. One minute it tells the pilot, *"Detecting imbalance. Compensating."* Then a minute later, *"Imbalance increasing."* And a minute later, *"Imbalance approaching handoff thresholds. In one minute, you will need to take control."*

His example shows that users need to understand trends, not just the working or not-working status of the agent. The example illustrates how this can be an audible concern notification, as discussed in Chapter 7, but this will need to become information that is easily glanceable, leading up to and possibly persisting throughout the handoff scenario.

High-Information Alarms

When things are trending poorly, a critical agent has called for takeover, and it has not happened, then the agent will need to sound an alarm. Of course, the primary signal should be attention-getting since that's what it needs, but its alarm can play a part in a successful takeover. Consider adding as much information to the alarm as necessary, to prompt the right response by the right person. If possible, identifying particular individuals to respond will avoid the *bystander effect*, in which no one responds because they think surely someone else has done so. It's useful to have a smart queue of alternate users ready at hand to directly ask to takeover.

Persistent Maps with Highlights

When someone takes over, they need to build an awareness of the situation as efficiently and effectively as possible. Don't hide this information beneath modal interfaces or even conversational interfaces, as these could cost valuable time. It's better to have a set of familiar maps in familiar places with glanceable information. And even more importantly, help direct their attention to the problem, what action needs to be taken, and what options there are, if known.

Assistive Cues

The agent will probably not just turn off during a handoff, but is much more likely to keep monitoring the situation, doing the things it can do with full confidence, and helping where it can. Detailing the assistive cues is beyond the scope of this book, but it is useful to note that unless it's the agent itself that has gone off the rails, it can still participate during critical handoff.

Emergency-Affordance Controls and Visuals

Much attention is given to the careful visual styling of software in terms of the brand, and agents should be no exception when they're running smoothly. But in emergency situations, branding should be thrown robustly out the window in favor of instant affordance and recognition. If the agent needs the user to grab the steering wheel, that fact should be apparent in milliseconds, because the user may not have much more time.

Takeback

Much more needs to be said about the *handoff* scenario, as this is when things are pear-shaped, but you must consider the takeback scenario as well, when the user hands full control back to the agent.

Signaling Readiness

As noted previously, the agent should continue to track variables and the stability of the situation during the handoff to see whether it thinks it can take full control again. When it can, it might need to do so automatically without asking the user's permission. This might be OK in a careening car with a panicked driver, but it might be very dangerous to try and take control of a scalpel in a surgeon's hand. If the takeback makes sense to be manual, the agent should clearly signal its readiness to the user.

Agreement

If the user must manually agree to hand back control, once the user understands that the agent can take back control, the user should signal his agreement. Whatever this control mechanism is shouldn't interfere with the primary task, and it's important to keep in mind that the user is or has just recently been managing a critical situation. Asking a driver to press a button on the far side of the dashboard to request takeback, for example, is more dangerous than having the driver speak this intention as an answer to a question.

Making Sure Everything Is Cool

Finally, even as the agent takes control again, the user will be in a heightened state and want to make sure that things are cool. Give the user a little reassuring span where he can keep his hands at the ready, see the performance and confidence of the agent, and let him rebuild confidence in the system, breathe, and let his heart rate return to normal.

Recap: Handoff and Takeback Are the Achilles' Heel of Agentive Systems

Agents have been shown to make their people less capable at the agent's task. This may not be a show-stopping issue in your domain. (See Chapter 10, "Evaluating Agents," for more on this.) If it's not, you'll have several considerations to take into account as you design the handoff and takeback of the task between the agent and its person.

- **Handing off to an intermediate:** Ensure that signals are clear and assurances are comforting when control shifts to an intermediate. (Note that you will have handoff and takeback problems with the intermediate.)

- **Practice:** Determine if the system warrants routine, live, or virtual practice. If it does need some kind of practice, design the regulation of that practice and what assistive help you can provide during practice.

- **Handing off to the user:** Warn the user when he might need to take over for a while. During this handoff, inform him about the state of the system, the nature of the problem, and the known options for a solution. While the user is in control, try to make the agent perform as a helpful assistant. Design controls to hand control back to the agent such that the handoff is smooth and the user feels confident.

- **Takeback:** Determine if the agent should take back control automatically as soon as it can, or if it should be a manual process. If manual, allow the user to instigate the takeback without affecting the task. Have the agent provide assurances when everything's back under control and follow up with the steps that can be taken to help prevent a similar event in the future.

CHAPTER 10

Evaluating Agents

In the previous chapters of Part II, "Doing," I've tried to lay out the aspects of an agentive technology that are unique to their design, as opposed to a more traditional tool-like system of design. But any good design practice should help you take stock of what you have wrought. To that end, you should consider what the right tools are for evaluating agents to know whether they're working for people. Let's talk about what methods might be appropriate and then go over what heuristics should be used.

Does This Mean No UI?

You'll note that, most of the time a good agent just does its thing and comes back with results. That does *not* mean that good agentive technology is free of the unbearable lightness of interface. Actually, they are chock-full of interfaces: interfaces for signing up and setting up. Interfaces for testing and launching, receiving notifications, and handling exceptions. Interfaces for play. Some agentive technology will have no user interfaces, but these will be rare and tightly constrained. When we get to general artificial intelligence, we'll have to revisit that assumption, but until then, users will need interfaces of some sort to help manage and collaborate with an agent, and those interfaces bear evaluation.

Methods

Many of the methods traditionally employed by usability, interaction design, and service design are applicable to agentive technology. The main challenges are that agents often play out over long periods of time or in response to unpredictable triggers. Contrast that with a usability test, which is often conducted in a highly controlled setting. Imagine trying to assess Betterment's roboinvestor—which is meant to play out over decades, responding to vagaries in the stock market and the user's life—over the span of 60 minutes in a lab setting, and you get a sense of some of the challenges.

As with other products, the best feedback comes from real users trying to work the product into their lives. The deliberate and focused nature of the usability test will skew results toward the immediate and should be interpreted as such. But you don't need to throw out the baby with the bathwater, just be aware of and compensate for its bias.

For In-Progress Agents

For designs-in-progress, designers can build *experience prototypes* to test with candidate users. These can be paper-and-pen prototypes for the traditional interface components, and person-behind-the-curtain for the agentive aspects. Either can be thrown together very rapidly.

For Mr. McGregor, we might mock up one of the scenarios described under handling exceptions—perhaps the "Just Blech" scenario from Chapter 8, "Handling Exceptions." We could share a similar task with a test subject, "You'd like to tell Mr. McGregor that you dislike kale and no longer wish to grow it," and ask them to figure out how to do it with paper prototypes or a quickly-comped digital prototype. Although they are a rough approximation, these experience prototypes will provide some feedback about the design.

> **NOTE** FAST, FAST, FAST PROTOTYPES
>
> Daniel Burka of GV (previously called *Google Ventures*) once helped test the Relay robot for hotel deliveries with an operator in the next room hidden from view of the test subjects, rather than using real agentive tech, and it took one business week, or five days. The GV book *Sprint: How to Solve Big Problems and Test New Ideas in Five Days* (Simon & Schuster, 2016) is one resource for how to build these experience prototypes quickly and effectively.

For Live Agents

Live agents have the benefit (and risk) of using the real product. The agent should be developed such that real usage metrics are available for hard data. This can guide understanding, but to understand why users are behaving the way they are, researchers should additionally have direct ethnographic research with people using the agents. As with traditional qualitative methods, an interview should be combined with observation to see if there's any difference between what they say (and what they think you want to hear) and what they actually do. Lab tests can still be done with live software, but you will almost certainly need to engineer an example trigger to mimic the oft-times unpredictable triggers that happen in the real world.

These techniques are not novel. They are well-heeled methods in user-centered design practice. But these descriptions should help you select the right methods from the many that are available to you.

Traditional Usability for the Traditional Parts

For each scenario that we're concerned about, users are performing tasks. Sure it's in the service of not doing tasks, or rather having the agent do it for them, but they are still interfaces and the body of methods and principles the industry has developed over decades of study and practice should be enough to cover these aspects of the design.

Trying to summarize the vast body of knowledge on usability testing is beyond the scope of this book, but it's worth mentioning that the heuristics mentioned next are in addition to, not *in lieu* of, these more traditional methods.

Heuristic Evaluation for the Agentive Parts

We also need to test the agentive aspects of these systems as well, and that requires some additional evaluative tools. As noted earlier, traditional usability isn't likely to serve us well for these parts. Fortunately, we have another category of tools to use, and that's heuristics. What follows are a suggested starting list of heuristic rules to test against.

The Results

The first line of inquiry has to be the most basic, and that's to see if the agent did what it was supposed to do. Did it trigger on the right things (true positives, in the language of Chapter 8)? Did it avoid the right things (true negatives)? The agent itself won't know this. It's a computer and can't escape its own limited model of the world. For it, every positive is a true positive. To answer this question, an external auditing system needs to be brought in and verify the agent, and any anecdotal evidence should be noted, too.

Secondarily, you need to make sure the agent performed as it was specced to. Did it apply the brakes *in time*? Did it help investors achieve their financial goals *better than the selected index fund*? Are the rows of seedlings *straight and evenly spaced out*? This might be measured by the agent, but may take external measurements or qualitative inquiry by a researcher to uncover.

User Confidence

The next line of inquiry is subjective and requires qualitative research to answer the question: "How *confident* do you feel in the agent?" This is important because the agent is working on the user's behalf. Confidence breaks down into several subquestions, which can be answered in a user survey with *Likert-scale* formats, which are those five-point scales that ask you to rate how you feel about a statement from strongly disagree to strongly agree.

- I'm confident that the agent performs when it is supposed to.

- I know when the agent is working and when it isn't.

- I understand what it's doing when it's working and can tell its progress.

- I think the agent will perform as instructed the next time it needs to.

- The agent only contacts me when it is necessary.

Note that more specific confidence questions would be more specific for a given domain. For instance, researchers looking into the user confidence of Mr. McGregor could ask users to rate the sentence, "I'm confident that Mr. McGregor keeps track of the health of my plants."

If an agent is performing well, and the user doesn't have confidence in it, then the agent is not conveying enough information about itself and its progress to the user.

Perceived Value

Separate from confidence, each user must decide whether or not using the agent is worth the money, the hassle, or the changes it brings with it. After all, I'm confident that AutoCorrect works, but I'm still not satisfied with it. Don't forget to ask, after all is said and done, to look in the aggregate for people who stop using or turn off the agent. Reach out to these users, especially to understand why they were unsatisfied. For users who do continue to use it, you can presume they are satisfied, but understanding why they are will help you keep true to those things that work as you improve the rest of the agent.

Cooperation refers to two things. First, many agents, especially as agentive technology becomes more ubiquitous, will need to cooperate with people, but also with other agents and computer systems. It will make requests of them, and they will make requests of it, regarding activities, information, or shared resources. If these are not handled well, the user will be dragged into becoming a technical manager of the conversations of agents, and this should be an issue for the providing organization rather than the user.

Secondly, nearly every agent needs to make accommodations for users who want to play alongside, direct, or even take control of the agent's triggers and behaviors. The agent needs to be responsive to direction and be able to pass into an assistive mode at any time without disrupting either the agent's tasks or the user's goals. Covering the patterns of assistive technology is also beyond the scope of this book, but should be considered since it is a known companion mode to agentive technology.

Measured Value

As noted in Chapter 7, "Everything Running Smoothly," the actual value that an agent provides may be obscured by the fact that users are most conscious of agents when the human needs to help the agent, that is, when the agent is failing. The risk is that these touchpoints unduly influence the user to think that the agent is just one massive pile of failure.

So, if possible (and meaningful), you should also use real data to paint a fuller picture than the subjective and compare this to data for users without the agent.

Does Spotify make music enjoyment and discovery easier and better than listening to the radio or of being your own DJ? Does ShotSpotter get faster, more consistent police responses to gunshots than just a citizen reporting alone? Does your text-composition-speed-per-letter increase or decrease with AutoCorrect turned on?

Ideally, the agent itself would be able to provide this information for the individual and for the aggregate of the people like the user, but if not, testing should include some way of measuring the value the agent provides. Control data from users or organizations not using the agent may be helpful for the comparison.

Recap: Evaluate with Heuristics

Since sophisticated agents are different beasts than their tool counterparts, you must evaluate them differently. The parts of the user interface that involve traditional task-*doing* can be evaluated using familiar methods from user-centered design (not covered here). But for the rest, consider evaluating against a set of heuristics most appropriate to a task-*manager*.

- **The results:** Does it work when and how it is expected to? How well can the user predict and depend on it? How easily can it or users tune its behavior to be more in line with what is desired?

- **User confidence:** How confident is the user in the agent? Does the user feel the agent is informative and polite?

- **Cooperation:** How directable is the agent? Can the user take control or influence performance when she wants to, how she wants to? How well does the agent handle exceptions? Does it know its limits? How does it equip the person taking over a task? Does it cooperate well with other agents and computer systems?

- **Perceived value:** Does the user *feel* it is worth having the agent involved? How did it convey measured value to the user, to help frame perceived value?

- **Measured value:** From as objective a perspective as possible, how did the presence of the agent affect the system in which it participated? Was it ultimately for the better?

PART III

Thinking

If the first section of this book was persuasive, and the second pragmatic, this last section aims to touch on the forward-looking issues surrounding the notion of agents. How will our practice of interaction evolve to design for this kind of technology? What ethical questions arise? What should you be thinking about as you build more and more of them as part of the way we live our lives? They're heady issues, but important ones. In the last chapter, I'll make my call to action, my rallying cry for what I'm hoping you'll do with these concepts.

CHAPTER 11

How Will Our Practice Evolve?

The practice of design adapts to the thing being designed. Agentive tools are different, so our practice will evolve. We will need some new vocabulary, techniques for addressing new use cases, ways to convey our designs for these use cases to stakeholders and developers, and some new ways to test agentive technology. In this book, I've provided what I trust is a fine springboard for strategists, product owners, and design practitioners to get started. Still, I do have some ideas about what we'll be working on next, at a macro level.

First, We'll Be Selling the Concept

If you look at the state of the tech industry today, technology and design practices are firmly rooted in the creation of good tools. We observe people doing work in order to understand the problem. We design with scenarios and use cases of personas using the tool. We test prototypes and alphas by asking people to accomplish tasks as we take notes. We speak of the "experience" of use, which doesn't quite apply to agents. Or maybe it must apply differently.

Most of the clients I've had the opportunity to work with over the years ask for help designing *powered* tools that reduce the number of steps in a process, or *metrical* tools that help the user understand their task in an informational way, or *corrective* tools that help draw attention to when known business rules are being violated, as well as recommendations for recovering. But as we've seen in the examples listed throughout this book, the technology exists today to create smart agentive technologies. As designers, we often look to minimize effort while maximizing the results for the user, and this is the logical next step to bringing technology to bear toward that goal.

So, if an agentive solution is right for our users, and our stakeholders aren't asking for it, it will be up to us to introduce the concept and sell them on the idea. As individuals, we'll be adding vocabulary, anecdotes, and case studies to our conversational backpack in order to get good at bringing these stakeholders along with our thinking.

Then We'll Be Working on Making Agents Smarter

The examples throughout this book illustrate how agentive technology is already present in small ways in the world, but most are relatively new. As with any technology, early agents are small and buggy, and it will be our job simply to iron out the wrinkles. We will need to create better smart defaults and easier ways of building rules and exceptions.

Sometimes, the "smarts" mean matching users' mental models and making the hard trade-offs between competing choices. The Apple Time Capsule is an example. It's a wireless, agentive backup system for the contents of a user's hard drive. It's meant to be as simple to use as possible, in that once it is turned on, it does all the backing up with an interface that presents a stack of file menus that get older as it goes back in the distance. But it's not actually an archive. It has an hourly backup of the last day's activity, daily backups of the prior month, and weekly backups for anything older. It keeps weekly backups until the disk fills up, and then it gets rid of older stuff. But that's a computer's way of thinking. It's weighing it by time and discarding *old*. If I'm counting on a backup, I have a different sense of prioritization. Pictures and videos of my son's birth are worth much, much more to me than the latest CDs I've ripped to FLAC, regardless of how old those images are. But to give users intricate controls means sacrificing simplicity and degrading the experience—until the agent can get very, very smart about it.

Sometimes, the "smarts" are in making agentive algorithms more humane, giving them at least the same consideration that a human would. The Facebook 2014 *Year in Review* is an example. As most know, in late 2014, Facebook surprised users with an automated Year in Review feature. In it, Facebook's algorithms looked at each user's server statistics to determine which pictures had gotten the most comments, and then presented a series of automated posts in the user's feed, featuring those images in illustrated frames. Some of those frames included balloons and streamers, evoking a party.

This feature worked well for most people, but it was devastating for anyone whose photos bore so many comments because they were about the death of a loved one or a bad breakup. On his blog, meyerweb.com,[1] Eric Meyer shared a screencap from his Year in Review, which featured a portrait of his daughter who had died. (Not shown out of respect.) He understood that he was just being subjected to a fantastically insensitive algorithm, but it still unexpectedly reopened his grief, framed in balloons and streamers.

Of course, this was an implementation oversight. Facebook could have made it opt-in only. They could have done very basic parsing of the words in the description and comments to glean the general

sentiment of comments, and if it was anger or condolence, exclude that image entirely. They could have parsed the year's status updates, and if the sentiment was negative, simply wish those users a brighter 2015. By February 2016, they seemed to have learned all these lessons with their Friend's Day campaign.

These kinds of critiques and suggestions are easy to deliver in hindsight. It's getting things right in the first place that is difficult, and we're going to be making these mistakes over and over again as we introduce new kinds of agents.

1 Meyer, Eric. "Inadvertent Algorithmic Cruelty." *Thoughts from Eric*. N.p., 30 Dec. 2014. Web. 10 Feb. 2017.

Hopefully, We'll Work on Having Them Fade Away

Many agentive projects I've personally worked on over the past two years have been services aimed at skills acquisition—kids adopting a healthy lifestyle, adults living deliberately, and investors learning to think long term. Even if, as designers, we made these "perfectly" smart (avoiding any Year in Review fiascos), we're faced with another problem, and that's that we don't want to be building a perfect crutch.

Kurbo is a service and award-winning app that teaches kids about healthier eating. I was one of the design team working on the project. The app starts with a training program with a real and a virtual coach that asks kids to track their meals while learning a "stoplight" system developed at Stanford to categorize foods, and then challenges them to reduce the number of "red" and "yellow" foods consumed over the course of the remainder of the program.

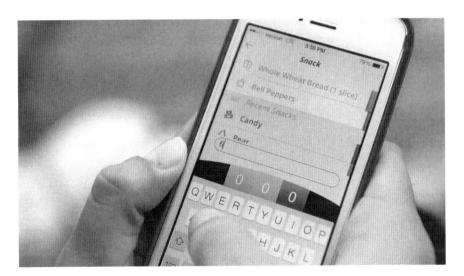

There were design challenges to making the training program fun and age appropriate, to helping the kids manage their social network in which food choices and weight shaming can play out, and even to making tracking meals as easy as possible since it happens every time you eat. But another major challenge was that some of the kids who improved their Body Mass Index while in the program would fall back to old habits afterward.

The crass solution is to try and get users hooked and dependent on a technology to continue their success. But Kurbo Health is a company on a mission to improve children's health, rather than just making a mad grab for people's attention. So we worked to ensure that the app continued to be fun and useful even after the training course was complete and the coaches went away. For example, there was utility, access to a sympathetic social network, and fun.

Many agentive services that offer to improve a skill set will need to be built in similar ways—as a scaffold that helps the user grow and then falls away as needed. This means we're not just *augmenting* humans. A crutch is an augmentation. Agents that know how to fade away will *improve* humans.

Recap: The Signpost Says AGI

Agentive technology will be a cutting edge of narrow AI while we await general AI. If general AI does come online, we won't need to design agents, or assistants, or automatons anymore. The AI will do it, and do it better than us. When will that be? Relying on the 2013 survey[2] conducted by Vincent C. Müller and Nick Bostrom, in which they asked hundreds of AI experts when we might expect AGI, we probably have the span of around 28 years from the publication of this book to continue getting good at agentive tech.

Median optimistic year (10% likelihood): **2022**

Median realistic year (50% likelihood): **2040**

Median pessimistic year (90% likelihood): **2075**

That sounds like a long time, but recall that software design as a stand-alone practice began in World War II, and we've slowly been improving tools and practices over the past seven decades. So, with that in mind, I suspect that propagating these three macro trends across the world of technology will fill up our time. I'll not try and forecast what might happen beyond that.

And, of course, the future is a funny thing. I could be wrong.

---

2 Müller, Vincent C. and Bostrom, Nick. 2014, "Future progress in artificial intelligence: A survey of expert opinion," in Vincent C. Müller (ed.), *Fundamental Issues of Artificial Intelligence* (Synthese Library; Berlin: Springer). www.nickbostrom.com/papers/survey.pdf. Accessed January 2017.

CHAPTER 12

Utopia, Dystopia, and Cat Videos

No technology is neutral. Not even the humble thermostat. It is apparent to any layperson that general artificial intelligence stands to transform culture in far-reaching and fundamental ways. It is frightening to consider that we don't know what life looks like should super artificial intelligence evolve. But what about agentive technology? What inherent biases does it have? How will it be abused? What does it afford? What does it want?

I'm only an armchair philosopher, so please forgive if this is less of a unified theory of agency and more of a collection of forward-looking questions and answers that have come up as I worked on, discussed, and wrote about agentive technology with people all over the world.

But before we get there, let me explain the title of the chapter. Genevieve Bell is currently the Vice President and Fellow at Intel leading the Corporate Sensing and Insights group. Over the past years, she and I have wound up speaking at a few of the same events. When I was at Interaction12 in Dublin, I saw her giving one of my favorite talks, in which she reviewed the predictions that came before the advent of some older technologies. Across several case studies, she noted that predictions tend toward the extremes: the coming technology will usher in either a new golden age, or bring about a new dark age, with little nuance in between. Her main example recounted some of the public predictions that came at the turn of the prior century about the new-fangled electric light. *gasp*

The Tyranny of the Light Bulb

On one side, you had some people at the time who were really excited about the coming age of light. Crime would disappear, the argument went, since we could easily illuminate every street, alley, and walkway brilliantly, giving the criminals nowhere to ply their dark trade. It would even mean universal education, since people could continue reading after the sun went down and there was no more work to do.

On the other side, you had some dire predictions as well. The working class would suffer greater exploitation since fat-cat business owners could illuminate their factories and eliminate sundown as an excuse to go home. Others worried that our circadian rhythms would fall out of sync with the sun and cause us no end of physical maladies.

Of course, now that we're over 100 years into electric light, each of these predictions seems naively extreme. It's more mundane than that. The truth ends up being somewhere in the middle. Crime doesn't like well-lit areas, but it didn't disappear because we didn't light everything all the time, and some crime happens just fine in well-lit places. It didn't mean universal education, because people had other things they wanted to do with the extra hours: like talking or playing parlor games. It wasn't *just* more reading.

Similarly, yes, factory interiors were illuminated, but it meant a more predictable work schedule throughout the year, so businesses and workers benefitted from the predictability. And factories weren't the only places illuminated. Nearby pubs were lit by electric light as well, giving those same workers the opportunity to socialize a bit with coworkers before heading home on roads lit by electric light, which was a decidedly positive addition to their days. And for circadian rhythms, well, OK, maybe that prediction was spot on. It's hard to say. I need a disco nap.

The sum effects of electric light weren't exactly neutral, either. It has enabled around-the-clock living, study, book-writing, and work. It enabled thicker and deeper buildings, with people squirreled away inside, cut off from natural sunlight. It drove the creation of our electricity infrastructure, which powered a great deal more than just light bulbs, and drove us to pollute more of the world. It added new shadows to our lives. It gave us movies and saved us countless minutes from having to stoke fires and light candles. It meant fewer things, you know, burning down. I can see positive and negative ways to interpret each of these effects.

But Will the Internet Save Us?

Bell recounts similar prediction patterns at the advent of the internet. Some predicted the complete loss of any sense of identity and a globally externalizing economy that would enslave us all. Others predicted the falling away of cultural differences and animosities since anyone could interact with anyone else around the globe at any time. A true golden age of peace. The reality, Bell notes, is much more mundane; we use this amazing worldwide connectivity machine to watch cat videos.

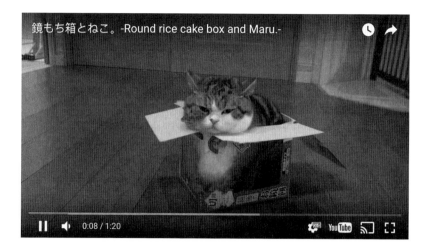
鏡もち箱とねこ。 -Round rice cake box and Maru.-

0:08 / 1:20

We should keep this recurring pattern in mind as we discuss agentive tech. Will the new age it ushers in be golden or dark? Although it has been around on factory floors and in computer science for a while, it still feels new to us. Our tendency may be to valorize or demonize it, when we should keep in mind that the truth will be something in between with much more nuanced—even if far-reaching—effects.

Dr. Jekyll and Mr. Agent

Let's start with the big one. Should you be *scared* of agentive tech? Will it tend toward evil? How might it be used for ill gain? Throughout most of this book, I've presented a progressive view, that agents will have a positive effect on the lives of their users. I'm a designer, by training: I want to make things work. But I'm also a skeptic, so let's take some time to consider how they might be used perniciously.

The definition and qualities of agentive tech provided in earlier sections give you some foundational things to consider.

- Agents are software, which acts on your behalf.

- That software monitors data streams and responds to triggers with rules.

- In the best cases, you tune it over time to be more effective and tailored for your needs.

Pull on the threads of these descriptions, and you can unravel some potential problems.

That it is *software* means it will come with all the problematic aspects of that medium. Notably, the majority of users of software cannot open it up to investigate what's inside, if they suspect some problem or malfeasance. Worse, agents often operate when they're out of your attention, and if they are doing nefarious things, you may not even know it. Imagine with our Mr. McGregor example, if thieves could hijack the agent and take control of the Bee drone to case houses in the neighborhood for potential marks.

Agents may not even need to be hijacked by criminals to behave in unsavory ways. In 2008, rumors began to circulate across the internet that the Apple "shuffle" algorithm felt less than random. David Braue of CNET ran a series of well-controlled tests on the software and showed that yes, it appeared that the "random" algorithm favored music that had been purchased from Apple's iTunes store rather than music that had been ripped from CDs, and it also favored artists from certain labels, notably Universal and Warner, presumably as a result of closed-door deals.[1]

Obviously, companies can control their message very precisely to avoid promising objectivity in their agent's behaviors, and as long as the effects are subtle, they will be able to get away with it. Imagine if the Narrative camera were programmed to favor images from the thousands taken across the day that included certain brands. Or worse, to insert those brands as subtly as possible in the images it took. Once I had iOS autocorrect the word "principled"—a perfectly valid English word that did not need correcting—to "Pringles,"—a brand name, and my first thought was, "Was this paid advertising?" Ethical product managers will need to take pains to prevent abuse of the algorithmic nature of agents and to ensure that their agents can be examined.

Deliberate malice may not even be the biggest concern. Any particular algorithm can formally encode the unconscious social or cognitive bias of its authors. You've probably already seen early face recognition from HP that couldn't recognize dark-skinned people, or Nikon's camera AI that asked photographers of subjects who had "double eyelids" if they were blinking after every single snap. I trust that neither is the result of deliberate malice on the part of the developers or the organizations, but the result is that the software is

---

1 Braue, David. "iTunes: Just how random is random?" cnet.com, August 4, 2008, 3:54 AM PDT. www.cnet.com/news/itunes-just-how-random-is-random/

biased, working well for some people and poorly for others. On the bright side, once encoded, these biases can be exposed, critiqued, and corrected, explicitly.

You might think that open-source agents are the answer, but general consumers won't have the programming expertise to understand what they saw even if they did look under the hood. But with open source, at least other experts (or other agents) would be able examine the code or run tests like Braue did, and raise the alarm for general consumers through social media or news channels. If, of course, consumers care. The furor over Apple's non-random shuffle was short-lived, officially denied, and then died down. iTunes is still out there.

It's not just the agents themselves that will be gamed. Once agents begin to have an effect on the marketplace, companies, depending on those effects, will do their best to *game the data* that drives the agent. Search engines and websites have long been in a "better mousetrap" arms race for most of the history of the web. If you're not familiar with these, programs called *web crawlers* go from website to website and "read" it to determine that page's content, quality, and relevancy to know how it relates to people's searches. Because being high in the search result is critical for some businesses, a whole profession of specialists has emerged to reverse-engineer the key attributes that those web crawlers are looking for. Then they heavily modify their web pages to match those attributes. In this way, these search engine optimizers are gaming the data that drives the web crawler. So, even if you could engineer open-source agents whose behavior holds no surprises, you still need to make sure that the data streams they monitor are as clean as possible. Which might mean more agents.

A last concern from the definition of agents comes from the idea that an agent becomes increasingly tailored to its user over time. That's good from the perspective of service, but it poses a risk. Sophisticated agents will slowly build a detailed model of their users. That can be a dark temptation to identity hackers. Even if the data an agent has is as simple as emails and calendar events like birthdays, gaining access to the agent's model of its user can be used to support more serious identity theft.

All told, the nature of agents poses some fairly serious threats via malicious actors. The security pressures on agents will be great. But I should note that not all agents can be misused. I'm not worried about either the Orbit Yard Enforcer or the Roomba. At least not in their current, well-constrained forms.

Ethics++

Because agents are causing changes in the world without in-the-moment human supervision, they raise serious issues of responsibility and ethics. When faced with an ethical dilemma, how should they behave? If they cause harm, who is responsible?

In a famous thought experiment called the *Trolley Problem*, first proposed by Phillipa Foot in 1967, a runaway trolley is on a track that will kill five people ahead of it. An observer has control of a switch that will veer the train off the first track and save the five, but kill a single person on the second track. Should the observer kill the one to save the five? This core scenario has seen many permutations to see how the changes affect ethical reasoning. While the original Trolley Problem was purely in the abstract, it has been increasingly brought to the forefront with the self-driving car.

The new question runs like this: If a self-driving car finds itself, despite all efforts at prevention, with a microsecond to choose whether to slam into an obstacle, risking the life of its passenger, or swerve onto the sidewalk, risking the life of a pedestrian, what should it choose? Does it do what most human drivers would do, which is to uphold obligations to its passengers? Does the decision rest on general policy (e.g., favor the pedestrian because they have no airbags) or—and this is much more disturbing—individual traits (e.g., favor the child over the nonagenarian, or vice-versa)? These are concrete questions, as the car must be programmed to do *something* in this circumstance.

The Academic Trolley

As rich as the conversations around Trolley Problems are, we must admit it is an academic problem. In the 1,000,276 autonomous miles logged by Google as of December 1, 2015, nothing like the Trolley Problem has come up. The answer seems, 99.99% of the time, to be just slam on the brakes.[2] Still, we want to have a generalized answer we can live with as we tackle other, similar problems.

If the tragic scenario results in a death or serious medical bills, there is also the question of accountability. Who is responsible? The rider, who selected the destination and told it to hurry? Or the security team that failed to prevent the hacker, who secretly thwarted the prevention algorithm? Or the manufacturer, whose component failed and got people into this situation? Or the developer, who coded the switch statement that told the car what to do? Or the company that sold the agent to the rider? There will be actual lives and millions of dollars at stake. Fortunately, some providers, such as Volvo, Google, and Mercedes-Benz have already stated publicly that they will assume liability for the performance of their cars.[3] Will this become the norm or law for providers of agents?

If you can create agents that operate rationally and according to plan as individual algorithms, how do they perform as a *system*? There have been stock market agents that began to respond to each other, creating a snowball effect that threatened to bring down the market before humans could diagnose the problem and unplug the machines. Who is responsible for these positive-loop interactions? How will designers safeguard against them? How will organizations police for infractions? How will the *police* police for infractions? Do they have the technological wherewithal to do so?

It is far beyond the scope of this book to try and answer these questions. There are entire fields of study emerging. One is called *roboethics,* and it's told from the designer's perspective. Another is called *machine ethics,* and it's framed from the robot's perspective. Each of these fields is dedicated to addressing these questions in their own way, and it's impossible to outline the considerations at play without digressing and greatly increasing the size of this work.

At minimum, we should first acknowledge that not all agents will be handling high-risk decisions. The makers of the Garden Defense Owl will probably never have to deal with them. But each designer should consider the issue carefully, and ask the questions of the agents they

---

2 McFarland, Matt. "Google's chief of self-driving cars downplays 'the trolley problem'." *The Washington Post.* WP Company, 1 Dec. 2015. Web. 15 Feb. 2017.

3 Cohen, Wayne, Esq., and Nicole Schneider, Esq. "Potential liability ramifications of self-driving cars." *Westlaw Journal Automotive* 36.3 (2016): n. pag. Web. 15 Feb. 2017. http://cohen-lawyers.com/wp-content/uploads/2016/08/WestLaw-Automotive-Cohen-Commentary.pdf

are designing. What possible damage can the agent cause? How does the system prevent the trolley circumstance, decide dilemmas, and remedy any damages it causes? As cultures operating within bodies of law, we must answer the question: Who is responsible?

Will Smarts Turn Machines into Slaves?

A related set of questions asks how much intelligence are you obliged to provide the car? Narrow AI may just perform simple math of known riders against detected humans in the path. But what if the car decided to save four pedestrians by striking a transformer box that cut power to a hospital, killing the people depending on life support? It made the "right" call based on what it knew, but in the big picture, it made the wrong call. Is that a crime of negligence on the part of the car provider? What if a competitor had better algorithms that did take such consequences into account? This pressure to make agents smarter so they make broader and better decisions has no upper limit, and may encourage an arms race of more and more sophisticated agents that amount to artificial general intelligence. What if a super intelligence makes a decision that seems bad on the surface, for example, "kill the pedestrians," and a jury can't believe the causality chain by which it reasoned that it had, in fact, saved thousands?

So there is an ethical pressure to make things smarter. But that has a flip side. The reason people are OK with having narrow AI do their bidding is that there is no apparent ethical problem with it. It's a machine doing what it was built to do. But as organizations respond to the pressure to make agents smarter, at what line do agents cross that philosophical line into personhood, and thereby become slaves, bound against will to servitude? The EU Commission has as of January 2017 begun to address the question of AI personhood from a conceptual and legal standpoint. Let's hope they and other organizations around the world can come to some agreement and put legal structures and cultural norms in place before it becomes a real problem.

An Uncanny Breach

Because they exhibit behavior and often use language, agents are likely to trigger anthropometric responses much more than their manual tool counterparts. That response will not *just* frustrate any users who expect the agent to have general intelligence. It could also be exploited to engineer all the "social engineering" hacks that thwart security now, taking advantage of our gullibility and politeness. Imagine a malware app that intercepts requests to Cortana and speaks in her voice, asking its user for some information to help it with an agentive task like, "Would you like help remembering anniversaries and birthdays? If you can grant me access to your contacts, we can set this up." Suddenly, the Cortana spoof has access to personal data it can use in its next phases of identity theft. (This would belong to a group of attacks including phishing (email), vishing (phone), and smishing (text), if you want to read more on it.)

Ethical designers will try and constrain the anthropomorphic response, but we will need a verifiable way to authenticate agents. In the farther future, we may even need a way to distinguish agents pretending to be people we trust. My security agent better be on the case.

Delivering Strict Services to the 99%

Agents are cheap compared to humans. A lot cheaper. Oh, and tireless. And for all practical purposes, infinitely replicable. Did I mention that they are ready to respond 24 hours a day? These aspects will be an overwhelming temptation for any profit-driven service provider to replace its human customer service reps with agents if it can. We've already seen customer service slip down the muddy slope of automated voice response systems, even though they can be infuriating, because the cost savings justifies the occasional infuriated customer. Fortunately, many companies still provide access to actual humans, but they work very hard to make them difficult to get to, to encourage self-service. We'll talk about what this "agentification" might mean for the job market later, but first let's talk about what this means for social stratification.

NOTE FOLK-HACKING

> Frustrations with automated voice response barriers have run so high that grassroots efforts have sprung up where people help each other get around the digital fences, with sites like gethuman.com and dialahuman.com. These sites catalog the semi-secret direct phone numbers or exact series of buttons you need to press to zip past the phone tree to get to a real live customer service representative. People hack the system just to talk to other people.

If you are a business having to pick where you should provide cheap-but-dullard agents and where you should provide expensive-but-robust human customer service representatives, the answer is pretty clear. The less profitable customers will get the agent. That means those customers will be dealing with systems that cannot do any general problem solving for them. To the point, rule bending is part of how people have long helped other people deal with their unique circumstances in light of fragile, authoritarian, or inflexible systems. *You forgot your wallet? Hey, it's no problem, I recognize you and know you're good for it. Just settle up next time.* On the negative side, this has led to bribe cultures, and we don't want agents to cough and show some sort of virtual palm just to do their job, but we also don't want to sentence the bulk of society to dealing with inflexible rules while the rich can get malleable treatment because they're dealing with humans. It might even be that dealing with a human instead of an agent becomes a status marker of conspicuous consumption, one of the unmistakable signs of luxury just because we know they're expensive.

Companies will try and encourage self-service through these agents, and do what they can to restrict access to the humans. And while we will try our hardest to make the agents as smart as we can, and as polite as we can, and as humane as we can, they won't be the same.

Disenfranchisement Without It

On the flip side of strict self-service, there are agents that grant their users a significant advantage. Agents are tireless, fast, and can be very smart in their domain. If the response time is critical to success, get yourself an agent. "Algo trading" is one of those domains, where its agents can keep tabs on data streams and social media, and then act within microseconds to purchase or divest itself of stock before any human or the market responds. In this case, having the agent isn't the detriment, like it is with services, but the advantage. In situations like these, you run the risk of disenfranchisement. In the future, will it be possible to do stock options trades without a software agent? Will access to the bot be gated by price? The algorithms these agents are working with are their advantage, so you know it absolutely won't be open-sourced.

Even if we're not talking about stock markets, consider agents for renters snapping up apartments in light markets like San Francisco or Singapore, tutoring agents that bring the best references and guidance to students, or hiring agents that can find the best-fit jobs and negotiate the best salaries. These each promise a marked advantage, and that means they can be sold at a premium. Can you avoid the arms race, or is it endemic to the marketplace? When you are considering what kind of society you want to have, you'll want to consider what playing fields you want to be even, like, say, schooling, and either constrain the use of agents, or ensure that everyone has access to the same ones.

Planned Robobsolescence

Robots will be inhabited by and coordinate with agentive software for their behavior and logic. Agents will be able to jump from robot to robot, device to device, and extend across many at the same time, depending on need. While this is valuable to keep continuity of provided service, it also means that the physical parts will become perceived as disposable components to the "real" thing. A ghost that doesn't rely on any particular machine. With hardware that is more prone to breaking down than software, this might prove a temptation for the robot and actuator providers to err on the side of cost over durability or recyclability, in turn adding broken and discarded components onto the already massive landfills that our technological lives have generated. Designers must consider the ecological costs to their hardware decisions.

How Many Agents Are Too Many Agents?

One of the things hinted at in the beginning of this chapter is that agents may well proliferate. How many might we end up with? Do I need to be accosted in the morning by my health agent, my commute agent, my money agent, and my family agent, all before I even make it to my toothbrush, toothpaste, and floss agents?

In his book *Enchanted Objects*, David Rose describes a world in which all the smarts of technology are embodied in techno-magical objects in the world around us. Umbrellas that catch our attention on the way out the door because it's going to rain. Desktop orbs that glow red when the value of our retirement portfolio is down. Cabinets that open to reveal telepresence portals to our loved ones. He presents this vision in explicit contrast to three other dystopias: a world covered with screaming screens, a world in which technology lives inside of us turning us into transhumanist cyborgs, and a world of social robots. He implicitly couples robots with the agents inhabiting them, and explicitly raises the specter that the world may be filled with far too many.

He presents a scenario of agent hierarchies that work much like the servant hierarchies of great houses of old. Yes, there may be a footman and a baker, but the lord of the house would primarily interact with the butler, who could ferry instructions or information to and from the other servants. That sounds like the ideal arrangement for the user, but suppliers of agents may not want an intermediate between their agent and the user, for the risk of being commoditized. Then again, maybe middleware agents will emerge to fill the need. These agents would be custom-built to interact with other agents rather than users.

This brings us, delightfully, to monkeys. In the 1990s, anthropologist Robin Dunbar noted a correlation between non-human primate brain size and the size of their tribes. The theory is that primate brains can only keep track of so many other individuals before they become overwhelmed, and this provides a cap to the size of a tribe. If the tribe grows too large, they become nervous or panicked, and fights break out. Either members are kicked out, or subgroups break off to return the tribe to a manageable size.

People have since extended the *brain:tribe* size ratio to humans, and hypothesized that given our primate origins and brain size, there might be some upper limit to the number of people for whom we can reasonably track their "interiority," their pasts and motivations. Everyone else must be objectified or treated transactionally. (The number is currently thought to be around 150 if you're curious.) When we add people to our social circles beyond that Dunbar limit, the theory goes, it means some others will necessarily fall out. Bringing it back to the topic at hand, will agents occupy a space in our minds akin to people? Maybe not, if their pasts and motivations are immaterial and subservient to our own. But if very sophisticated agents do take up slots, then we have a dark possibility. Agents stand to displace people, and we will want to minimize the number of agents to which we are regularly exposed.

NOTE CHARLIE, THAT REALLY HURTS

Note that agents may already be working to squeeze out more Dunbar room for themselves. There is an app *Charlie* that looks at your calendar and, a few hours ahead of any meeting, sends you summaries of all the news items and fruitful topics of conversation related to the people you'll be meeting with. That way you can ask them, say, how things have been at their company since the merger. Most people will infer that since you know about the merger, you're interested in their business and lives, and that they're in your Dunbar circle, when really, it's an agentive patch. If you use Charlie, you don't have to track people, you just have to track Charlie.

I wonder, though, if highly constrained agents, especially those that don't use language, may occupy a spot more like a pet or a farm animal, if they occupy a spot at all. Although I don't know any studies that deal with how many "slots" of the Dunbar limit a pet occupies, I suspect it is less than a person. We should do studies to answer that question. But if the agents we build can coordinate among themselves, then we will need to admit the possibility that our agent will be demoted and managed through another intermediary agent at some point.

Designers of agentive systems should take this into account. Do you want to encourage or discourage the notion of your agent's person-hood? Whichever you pick, how will you make it clear?

Will We Lose the Skills We Hand Over to Agents?

One of the most common questions I get when I present about agentive technology (and you should mention me to the nearest conference organizer at once) is whether we'll lose the skills that we hand over to agents. The short answer is, even if we ameliorate some skills with routine practice, yes. Anytime we stop performing a skill, we stop being as adept at it.

The longer answer is: mostly. Some skills don't take constant practice. Casual bike riding is a canonical example. *It's just like riding a bike.* But managing high-performance tasks or edge-case problems on that bike, like racing across a mountain trail, *does* become more difficult without practice.

Still there's nothing that says that the user can't continue their practice right alongside the agent. Imagine a sports photographer who keeps her camera clicking even while her drone flies around doing the same thing. While it kind of goes against the ultimate utility of agentive tech, it's entirely reasonable to imagine that the photographer might engage the agent as a fail-safe. That frees her up to take more risks, because even if they don't pan out, she has the agent's tried-and-true results to fall back on. I'd argue that means that the photographer will get better at her craft for having the agent in the mix.

Still, I imagine that will be an exception case. Mostly agents will be used not as a fail-safe, but as a primary task-doer. What about those skills? Will we lose them?

Keep in mind that even in the modern world, many "antiquated" skills are maintained by a small subset of people in the culture because it satisfies them or there is still a demand. Photography didn't obviate painting; painting just became an expressive art. Factory production didn't obviate shoe making; cobblers just now target wealthy patrons. Self-driving cars won't obviate driving; driving will just become a thing some weird people do in their spare time. In the 1995 sci-fi novel *The Diamond Age* by Neal Stephenson, he envisioned a society in which nanotech construction became so commonplace that handmade objects were a status symbol for the wealthy, which in turn drove demands for those goods, which in turn drove further mastery of the skill. Sure it's fiction, but it seems a telling fiction. So while most individuals may lose skills, the culture as a whole may not.

There's another way that agents may help us not lose skills. We can imagine sometime in the future, narrow AI may learn skills before they completely die out in the population. Doris McLemore is at the time of writing, the last living speaker of the Native American language Wichita. If we could build a language-learning agent, then we might be able to capture some of this language's richness before she passes. We will lose her, but we may be able to keep the memory of her, her language, and her culture, and in that way, not "lose" the skill as we might have before.

The deeper answer to the original question is that we have been making this trade-off for a long time. Do you eat bread? If so, do you know how to sow, farm, reap, separate, and mill the wheat? The overwhelming majority of people reading this book can't, and that's because we have a technology we call "society." Members of this society specialize on one practice, to optimize their earning potential, and they trust that all the rest of the things they need to live will be available in the market.

Few people would assert that if you are not a farmer, reaping wheat is a critical modern skill, but nearly everyone depends on it all the same. This seems obvious when you are talking about skills you don't have, but it feels more unsettling when you consider skills you've personally spent a lifetime practicing. Driving, for instance. It feels weird to think that my young son may never learn to drive, but then I ask myself why it was necessary in the first place. Can he live a good life without putting his hands to the wheel? I'd say of course, and in the future, even more so. It feels even weirder when you consider skills with life and death at stake. Future agents may be better at surgery than any human, but I can't imagine going under that knife until it has decades of success under it.

Some curmudgeons will lament that this means that the young generation is just getting dumber because they don't know some "basic" skills. But I don't think so. They may not learn what we know, but it doesn't mean they know *less*. The parts of the brain that used to be dedicated to "how to drive" will be "spent" on learning other skills. They will be learning different things, like how to manage a small army of agents, and to get more done with fewer resources. They will be learning to manage the complexity of the world that they have inherited from their forebears. We can barely imagine the skills it will take to navigate their world. And they'll do it with at least as much aplomb as we had managing our world. If we do our jobs right, they'll do it with more.

It may be that the skills we lose by handing them to agents are just part of the evolution of society. We shifted a lot of work to machines at the Industrial Revolution, and even more at the start of the Computer Revolution. We are shifting more work to agents as time goes on, and we will again at the Artificial Intelligence revolution, should it finally come.

Are We Setting Ourselves Up as Dependents?

This is the darker side of the same question.

As described in Chapter 3, "Agentive Tech Can Change the World," ShotSpotter listens to microphones in a neighborhood for gunfire and pinpoints the exact location of any shots fired within seconds, greatly reducing response times for officers. But ShotSpotter does not (yet?) give any report to citizens in that neighborhood. Once they see ShotSpotter work a few times, will they presume they no longer need to report gunfire? When they lose that sense of responsibility, what happens when the service is down and shots are fired? Do criminals just get carte blanche until the agent is working again? In this case, we could solve the problem by telling citizens when shots have been detected and officers are on their way. But not every problem of dependency on agents has an obvious answer.

I'm comfortable shifting some of my life maintenance chores to other humans, partly because they are, in turn, depending on me. Agents have no default reciprocity or empathy. I'm also comfortable trusting other humans because we have a general intelligence. If an earthquake hits, we can all help each other to figure out the new landscape, recover, and get back on track. But offloading to narrow artificial intelligence is different. By definition, it doesn't have the general intelligence to handle wholly new situations, and so it is a shakier ground on which to build a civilization. This makes dependence on agents a riskier thing. What happens when people lose the skill of driving, the autonomous car network is down, and someone needs to get someone else to a hospital? What happens when we need to grow our own food, farmbots have been hacked into dysfunction, and no one remembers how to grow crops? What happens when we need to send a letter rather than an email, and the postal service has been dismantled due to disuse? Society will fail less elegantly, which is a polite way of saying there will be difficulty, suffering, or possibly death. Pushing toward general AI is one tactic, but it's hard for designers and product managers to contribute directly to that cause. But we *can* ensure that the practice and handoff capabilities are built into any agentive technology we help create, and that those capabilities are well and robustly designed. How this scales is a tougher problem we'll need to solve.

Do They Let Us Blind Ourselves?

The results of the United States presidential election in 2016 came as a surprise to almost everyone who was involved. Even professional forecasters had it completely backward. Don't we live in a massively interconnected world? Don't we know everything? How did the results come as a surprise?

Many fingers, including those of Matthew Ingram of *Fortune* magazine, point to social media and particularly Facebook to explain the surprise. By giving us the ability to mute and block voices we don't like, users tended to create networks of like-minded people and were thereby exposed only to familiar ideas. But even if you were a civic-minded user who welcomed and engaged opposing voices, Facebook's newsfeed was working against you. The newsfeed is an agent that trolls the thousands and thousands of possible items it could show you to determine what it will fit into your limited attentions, and it did so by showing people what pleased them. For a long time, the only thing you could do was *like* an item. More recently, changes were made to allow a user to register other reactions, but there wasn't a good way to tell it why, and there was not a clear way to explain what you *did* want to see and why.

This presents a major challenge to creators and designers of technologies, because it implies that there are bad consequences to just letting users set up critical systems in ways that please them. With the built-in human foible of confirmation bias and our seeking to avoid the unpleasantness of cognitive dissonance, we will tend to create the same filter bubbles where we get comfortable affirmation rather than challenging information. Now understand that the tools we design for users to modify an agent's triggers and behaviors are exactly that—ways to create more pleasing agents. (See Chapter 8, "Handling Exceptions.") For physical tasks, this might not be troubling, but for news and information tasks, it is.

In Chapter 3, I spoke about the concept of *drift* in the much more neutral domain of recipes. Drift is how an agent can encourage users to step outside of their known preferences to discover new things. Could that include more than food? Could it include concepts? Political views? Could it encourage building a bigger picture of the world around them?

Will We Lose Our Jobs to Agents?

In the summer of my fourth year as an undergraduate, I worked for the Texas state government. The job was to go around Harris County and document services available to indigent communities, including what the particular service was (food, shelter, job training, counseling, babysitting), times of operation, requirements, restrictions, phone numbers, addresses, etc. I then had to write them up in a consistent and digestible format and compile them into a three-ring binder, which was then copied and given to county social workers to use when working with their clients. If it needs to be stated at this point, my job that summer was to be a search engine.

I tell this story to remind us that, yes, we lose jobs to technology. We always have. But also to note that this isn't always a bad thing. Modern search engines are many orders of magnitude faster than I was, more thorough than I was, and the information was more up-to-date and useful than the three-ring binder I produced.

Looking back, losing this job to technology seems obvious in hindsight. It's harder to look at the current world and admit that some of the jobs held by skilled and experienced people will go away. What will we do with all the truck drivers, portfolio managers, and book authors once those tasks are handled by some version of artificial intelligence? Over the past decades, most societies have been able to retrain and reabsorb the people who held jobs that had become obsolete. We didn't just put switchboard operators out to pasture. But given the massive technological infrastructure much of the world enjoys now, the threat is that the coming replacements will happen much more rapidly—too fast for us to deal with in the same ways we've done before. What can we do?

We can try to build better, faster retraining mechanisms. We should do that anyway. But we can't rely on just that tactic.

Others like John Markoff, author of the 2015 book *Machines of Loving Grace*, argue that we should focus our efforts on human augmentation rather than human replacement. In the parlance of this book, he's admonishing us to focus on assistants and not automation. I'm not sure where agents would fall in his estimation. At the same time they empower us to "do" tasks without really doing them, we are removing the opportunity for a human to offer to do the same thing.

Still others look even broader and push us to ask the largest questions we can about civilization: Do we need to rethink the notion of work? Are we at a high enough productivity rate that we can produce enough with the resources we have that we can let people choose whether they want to work at all? That raises all sorts of questions about incentives, inequality, efficiency of markets, and more, but some smart people have thought of all of this and come up with the answer of yes. Look into the writings around *universal basic income* and *job mortgages* if you'd like to learn more.

Whatever our response, we should get ahead of it. It's hard to imagine, with the economic forces at play, that an agentive revolution is *not* coming. We should not let it blindside us.

What Will Agents Do to Our Self-Perception?

Sigmund Freud once noted that humanity's collective ego has historically suffered several massive demotions. Let's recount some of them.

At one time, we frolicked along, believing that we were the center of the universe, with the stars, sun, moon, and planets revolving around us in, OK, sometimes-convoluted ways. *Oh wait,* Copernicus stopped our frolic to demonstrate, *it turns out we are not the center of the universe.* The moon may orbit us, but we and the other planets orbit the sun. Other planets have moons, too. Since then we've learned that we aren't even near the center of our own galaxy. The sun orbits the center of the galaxy. In Douglas Adams' words, "Far out in the uncharted backwaters of the unfashionable end of the western spiral arm of the galaxy." Oh yeah, and this is one of 400 billion galaxies in the observable universe. So far.

Well, our ego thought, *rubbing its forehead, at least we're the pinnacle of the animal kingdom.* Not so fast, interrupts Darwin, removing his furry costume. We aren't perfect specimens of almost anything. There are animals with better perception, brain size, more endurance, use of language, peaceful natures, altruism, and even biological immortality. We are the fittest only for some definition of our current ecological niche, carrying a lot of painful evolutionary baggage, the happenstance of a process that is semi-random. We are not the end-state of any grand design, but the lucky leaves on a weird bush that is still growing and changing across geologic time. The roaches may outlive us.

Well, we are God's special children, right, our ego asks, rooting around in the liquor cabinet for the most-proof anything? But worldwide communication, easy insight to other cultures, and comparative religion take the shot glass from ego's hand to reply that, well, it depends on which of the thousands of documented gods you ask. If you believe in one or even a small handful, you deny the reality of the thousands of others, as well as the reality of their worshippers. So, we're only a god's special children if you choose to be an atheist to those others, and presume you happened to be born at the exact right time, place, culture, and family who picked the one true religion with the right story that told you that you were a beautiful and unique snowflake.

At least we're the masters of our own mind, our ego says as it rocked in a corner, hugging its knees and staring into the darkness. Well, hang on, says Freud, emerging from and possibly as the darkness. Given psychoanalysis, he says, we are not the masters of our own mind. We are subject to forgotten influences and post-hoc justifications of our subconscious desires, unable to tame either our sexual instincts or trust the perceptual mess that gives rise to our sense of reality. Our consciousness is merely a justification engine for what our subconscious decides we are going to do.

Poor ego, wherever it is now.

In addition to these dark demotions from being the bright center of the universe, now we are faced with the fact that we have created technology that can drive cars better than us with fewer accidents and greater efficiency. We have devices that can manage our life maintenance chores more routinely and thoroughly than us. We have software that can play *Go* better than us. They might also eventually run the planet better than us—more ecologically with fewer wars, less disease, hunger, and inequality. Are they better at stacking the odds toward our own long-term sustainable happiness?

Where does that mean we are in the scheme of things? The disposable cocoon from which this superior intelligence emerges? What does this mean to our sense of self? To our sense of how to spend our time on this planet?

More than any of the other issues I've raised so far, I'm at a loss to derive any imperatives for us as product managers and designers as we pursue agentive tech. It may be as cold as to acknowledge it and wish us all good luck with the therapy.

Is This as Close as We Ought to Come to General AI?

The Fermi Paradox is a philosophical and scientific question that asks why given the billions of galaxies we see and the ancient age of the universe, do we appear to be alone? Why doesn't the universe display the same explosion of life we have here on Earth? One theory posits that there is some Great Filter that ultimately destroys every intelligent species that comes into being. Some believe that artificial general intelligence *is* the specific self-destruction technology.

Maybe military AI eventually sours. Once we build drones and big robotic dogs to kill, will one bad system upgrade turn them into twitchy killing machines? Will someone write a computer virus to turn our weapons against us?

Will it come from unbounded optimization? Oxford philosopher Nick Bostrom, author of *Superintelligence: Paths, Dangers, Strategies*, first proposed a problem called the "Paperclip Maximizer" in 2003. He asked, in a thought experiment, what if someone instructed a general AI to gather as many paperclips as it could to the best of its ability. To follow that instruction, it might begin to buy, collect, and make them. To fulfill its remit, though, it should also improve its own capabilities to paperclip maximization, and evolve itself into a superintelligence that isn't driven with an ethical framework, just the desire to possess more and more paperclips. That optimizer might wrest metals away from other human endeavors, like city building. It might try to harvest the iron in human blood. It might convert the available matter in the solar system to an orbiting ring of paperclips.

Or is it just unassailable logic? We haven't managed to completely tame our brutal natures despite a history of trying. Should it ever gain sentience and open its eyes to evaluate humanity's place in the world, what will it conclude? Will it see us as its troubled progenitors to constrain and care for? Or will it see us as an infection or cancer ruining an otherwise functional ecosystem? Will it regard us *at all*, or dismiss us as we do animals, stupid biological things fine for subjugation and harvesting, but not of any real interest?

We might try to provide the general AI a hardwired ethical framework, but how are we going to do that? No human has yet described a code of ethics on which everyone can universally agree, and we have been trying for millennia, across cultures, and languages, and philosophies. What makes us think the programmers entrusted to write ethics into general AI will fare better? Considering this question, readers will almost certainly think of Asimov's famous Four Laws of Robotics.

0. A robot may not harm humanity, or, through inaction, allow humanity to come to harm. (Asimov added this "zeroth" law in 1950, 8 years after the publication of the famous first three, below.)

1. A robot may not injure a human being or, through inaction, allow a human being to come to harm.

2. A robot must obey the orders given it by human beings except where such orders would conflict with the First Law.

3. A robot must protect its own existence as long as such protection does not conflict with the First or Second Laws.

But if you read his stories, or the subsequent decades of critique, or the stories that have investigated edge cases where these laws might not work, or the additional proposed laws; it becomes clear these laws are far from complete. A top-down ethics still seems to elude us. It might seem hopeless.

I draw hope from the opportunities that agentive technology gives us in this regard.

In establishing the rules by which we want our agents to do work on our behalf, and more so in providing the tools by which users can create and modify their own rules, what are we ultimately creating? Don't think about one agent. Think about all the agents, their capabilities, and their rules. We will be building a giant, worldwide database of behaviors, rules, and contexts by which we want to be individually treated. That stack would be impossible for any human to make sense of, but it might be the exact right thing to hand to the first artificial general intelligence.

Maybe in working on triggers and rules, we're building the *Ultimate Handbook of Helping Humans,* one rule at a time. Agentive technology may be the best hope of ensuring that general AI doesn't end up being our Great Filter. Instead of four laws of robotics, we'll have four trillion laws of humanity.

Recap: Issue-Filled Issues

So as you can read, the notion of agentive technology is not neutral. It touches on our sense of selves, our economy, our ethics, even how we understand and affect the world. It's not just an evolution of our tools. Will it be a utopia, a dystopia, or just, you know, agentive cat videos? I won't pretend to have identified all of the ethical questions that agents raise, but I am confident this is an important first set. We could just solve the business problems that come our way, put agents out into the world, and see what happens. But if you're like me, you want to have a part in answering these questions by thinking through these issues and putting agents out into the world that try to make it right. The stakes are becoming increasingly large. That call to action is the next and final chapter.

CHAPTER 13

Your Mission, Should You Choose to Accept It

In the pilot episode of Joss Whedon's 2002 space western *Firefly*, to defend Serenity Valley against the wicked Alliance, the protagonist Mal steps onto an anti-aircraft weapon to shoot down an incoming enemy spaceship. As he grabs the handles of this weapon, a heads-up display crackles to life above the barrel of the weapon. The display has two crosshairs, also called *reticles*. The first is a fixed reticle, showing where the weapon will fire. The second is a glowing yellow, digital reticle, which shows where the bad guy is, tracking the spaceship in real time as it and the weapon move. As the audience watching this scene, we know instantly what Mal's job is. He has to move the digital reticle onto the fixed reticle, pull the trigger, fire the weapon, and save the day. As a narrative device, it frames the tension of the beat in an instant, and provides an exciting signal that this isn't just a western. It's a *space* western.

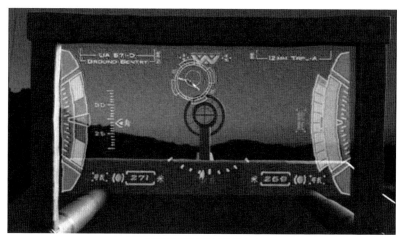

MUTANT ENEMY PRODUCTIONS

But as a designer who has spent the better part of a decade evaluating interfaces in science fiction as if they were in the real world, this had me pausing the playback and scratching my head. (And not just because it has a Weyland-Yutani logo at the top.) *Hang on*, I thought. *If the weapon knows exactly where the bad guy is, why does it wait for Mal to aim it?* Of course, we want a human to make the ethical decision of whether or not to pull the trigger, or at least to confirm that the bad guy is a bad guy. That's something I don't think we're comfortable relegating to machines. But for the *aiming*, the computer would be faster and more accurate than he is. It clearly has the data, and the circumstance is mission critical, so why doesn't it do the thing?

I suspect the reason is because this scene doesn't happen in the real world. It happens on television and computer screens. And in our entertainment, we really need our heroes to be heroic. That requires that they face difficult odds, use their cunning, skill, and imperfect tools to struggle, and eventually, yes, shoot down the spaceship and save the day. To me, this illustrates a telling discrepancy between our mental model of what makes for a compelling story and what technology is actually capable of to help us solve problems and achieve our goals.

It tells me that the challenge facing this evolution of technology isn't just *operational*. It's not just about applying the right technology to the right problem in the right way. It's also a *conceptual* one about what our role is in a world with technology that exhibits more and more agency, and how we talk about it with each other.

Presuming it was you and not your book-reading agent, thanks for coming with me this far. Across these pages, I've made the case that agentive technology is new (to us), promising, and distinct enough to warrant its own study. I've presented dozens of examples to show that it's out there and building momentum. I've shared some design ideas for a speculative gardening agent to illustrate the power of the idea. I've presented some first-draft patterns and heuristics from which you can draw and which you can iterate. I've raised the higher-order issues we should be considering as we continue to iron out the details.

If I've done my job and convinced you that agentive technology is one of the Next Big Things, awesome. Glad that worked out. But we still have work ahead of us.

We must shift our day-to-day practice from building tools for people to do work themselves to building usable, effective, and humane agents.

We must spread these models throughout the organizations in which we do our work of designing and developing things that help users achieve their goals.

We must figure out complementary models and patterns for *assistive* technologies. (I suspect the field of computer-supported collaborative work will have many answers.) We have to design our products elegantly to pass between these modes at the right time and in the right ways.

We must build a community of practice so that we can get better at this new work. To build a shared vocabulary amongst ourselves to have good and productive discussions about what's best. To share case studies, analysis, critiques, successes, and yes, failures. To get some numbers about effectiveness and return-on-investment to share with our business leads. To push these ideas forward and share new, better development libraries, documentation techniques, and conceptual models. To reify the ways we talk to others about what it is we're building and why.

Maybe this will happen in individual conversations over Post-it Notes, whiteboards, tablets, and beers. Maybe it will happen virtually. I certainly invite you to join communities beginning to form. I'll maintain a list of the ones I know about at agentive.ai for you to consider, and please let me know if you know of or start others. Maybe in the future, we'll have enough momentum to meet and chat about these things at a conference dedicated to it and to developing its community of practice.

It would be cool to meet you and get to talking about the evolution of technology, about the right thing to design and designing the thing right.

Let me close by telling of another scene from another sci-fi show. Early in the 2014 movie *Guardians of the Galaxy*, a bounty hunter named Rocket Raccoon uses some interesting technology to find his next mark among all the people crowding a public square. The device is a transparent rectangle that he holds out in front of his snout. It uses some smarts to recognize the person at the center of the rectangle and perform a quick database search to determine and display their value as a bounty. Rocket tests out a few people around the square but doesn't find anyone interesting. His attention is pulled away from this task by his partner, Groot, who is, much to Rocket's exasperation, drinking water from a public fountain. While Rocket talks to Groot, the device issues two tiny beeps. In response, Rocket looks through the device again, to have it direct him toward Peter Quill, our protagonist and a mark with a very high bounty on his head.

MARVEL STUDIOS

Overlooking Rocket's ethical ambiguity, what a marvelous and compelling image of an agentive technology. The beeps tell us that the device is looking for a high-value mark all the time, whether Rocket is paying attention or not. It is agentive. But it doesn't constrain Rocket to the role of babysitting an advanced algorithm. It lets him still try his tiny, furry hand, to see if he can beat the agent or find something it doesn't know about. It even lets him ignore it when other pressing matters present themselves, like reprimanding his goofy partner. It continues to let Rocket be Rocket, while still helping him achieve his goals.

This scene tells me that things are advancing. That people are thinking about this. There are a few new models out there to inspire us to this new way of interacting. That encourages us to see the opportunities of building and incorporating this new technology into our lives in ways that avoid either keeping us doing work just because we're used to doing it, or relegating us to being the background characters in some technology's story. It gives all of us a promotion from being task-doers to task-managers. To partnering with agents. To being more powerful and more human. To getting more done in our lives with less.

I look forward to the day when this won't be a remarkable scene to point out, but just the way our technology really *works* for people.

Consolidated Touchpoints

C hapters 6–9 describe touchpoints common to agentive systems. The diagrams in this appendix consolidate all the touchpoints illustrated at the beginning of those chapters into a convenient single place for easy reference. This first diagram organizes the touchpoints chronologically, in the order the user would likely encounter them. This is primarily useful to understand when different scenarios are likely to occur in relation to each other.

setup	running

Capabilities and constraints
Goals and preferences
Permissions and authorization
Test drive
Tuning tools
    A hood to look under
    Tuning triggers
    Tuning behaviors
Launch
Distributed customization

Pause and restart
Monitor
Notifications
    Suggestions
    Performance
    Completion
Exposed false negatives
Play alongside

problems	disengage

Notifications
    Resources
    Concern
    Problems
Simple manipulations
Tuning tools
    A hood to look under
    Tuning triggers
    Tuning behaviors
Handoff
Takeback
Practice

Disengagement check-ins
Death

This second diagram organizes the touchpoints along the see-think-do loop introduced in Chapter 5, "A Modified Frame for Interaction." This breakdown is useful partially for a division of labor. The touchpoints listed under *See* are mostly about user interface, visual, and microinteraction design. The remaining touchpoints are more likely to involve workflow, interaction, and industrial design.

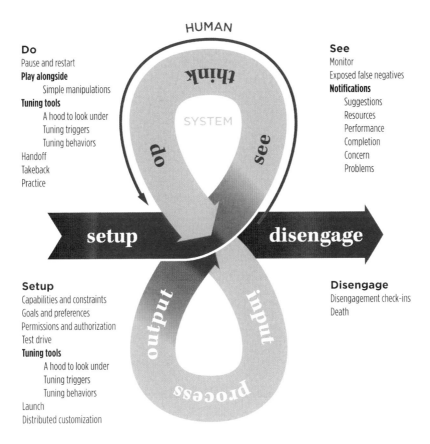

Do
Pause and restart
Play alongside
  Simple manipulations
Tuning tools
  A hood to look under
  Tuning triggers
  Tuning behaviors
Handoff
Takeback
Practice

See
Monitor
Exposed false negatives
Notifications
  Suggestions
  Resources
  Performance
  Completion
  Concern
  Problems

Setup
Capabilities and constraints
Goals and preferences
Permissions and authorization
Test drive
Tuning tools
  A hood to look under
  Tuning triggers
  Tuning behaviors
Launch
Distributed customization

Disengage
Disengagement check-ins
Death

A List of Referenced Agentive Technology

I mention a great many examples of agentive tech throughout this book, partly as an attempt to underscore that this sea change has already begun and partly to illustrate the broad applicability of the pattern. This appendix consolidates all the specific agentive technologies mentioned into one place for easy review. Each is listed in the order it appears. I have only included the "real-world" agents, omitting assistive or fictional technologies. If it needs to be said, this is not a comprehensive list of all agents in any domain. These examples are not necessarily first-to-market or even best-of-breed. Rather, these were selected for familiarity and their illustrative utility. If you are eager to bring other exemplary agents to my attention, please send a description to examples@agentive.ai, or, better yet, post it to social media with the hashtag #example and @AgentiveTech.

Chapter 1

Cornelis Drebbel's Incubator (c. 1597)

This egg incubator relies on a column of mercury to raise or lower a plug on a box filled with steam, to maintain a good temperature for the hatching of eggs.

Albert Butz's "Damper Flapper" (1885)

Like Drebbel's incubator, this heating system uses an analog feedback loop to monitor the temperature of a space, and when it gets too cold, opens the vents to a coal fire furnace to pipe in warm air.

Jewell Thermostat (1907)

This early wall-mounted mechanical thermostat includes a thermometer and a clock.

T-86 Round Thermostat (1953)

Henry Dreyfuss designed this wall-mounted mechanical thermostat, unifying the components into a single circular shape. The device is recognized in the Smithsonian design museum collection.

Nest Learning Thermostat (2011)

This much-discussed device is a wall-mounted digital thermostat with a well-designed display. It features a machine-learning algorithm that monitors many data sources and user preferences to keep occupants comfortable.

Chapter 2

Semi-Automatic Spell Correction (c. 2007)

Early spell-check was a word processing function, which users had to invoke. As processor speeds increased, spell-check became a persistent background function, underscoring questionable words as the user typed. Semi-automatic spell correction, as seen in modern versions of Microsoft Word, Google Docs, and iOS each take the extra step of automatically correcting misspellings and grammar mistakes in which it has a high degree of confidence. Users are shown a notification of the change and offered the opportunity to undo the correction.

x.ai (2016)

Once you grant access to your calendar(s), you can CC "Amy Ingram" and have the agent find the best time for a meeting between people with busy schedules. She provides options to your attendees and confirms the ones they've chosen. She will contact you again if there's a problem or after the meeting has been scheduled, and, of course, make a calendar reminder as well.

Pandora (2000)

An on-demand music listening and discovery service, Pandora bases its recommendations on seed playlists as well as users' listening history, matching them against a huge catalog marked up with thousands of attributes.

Spotify (2006)

Like Pandora, Spotify is an on-demand music listening service additionally notable for its beloved and much-touted Discover Weekly suggestions. These new music recommendations are algorithmic and based on listeners' microgenre taste profiles, similar-listeners' playlists, and even natural-language parsing of playlist titles.

Google Alerts (2003)

This agent lets users describe search terms for Google to run persistently, emailing users any time that new results appear.

Naïve Bayesian Spam Filters (c. 1998)

Rule-based email filtering can be as easy as moving anything with the word "Unsubscribe" to the trash. Bayesian spam filtering is more sophisticated. It relies on finding any of a set of keywords in the text to calculate a confidence whether a given message is spam. Anything over the threshold gets dropped into a spam filter. Anything under gets passed through to the inbox. An academic description of this technique first appeared in M. Sahami et al. (1998) "A Bayesian approach to filtering junk e-mail," AAAI'98 Workshop on Learning for Text Categorization.

Chapter 3

iTunes Follow (2015)

As part of its digital music platform, Apple provides fans with the ability to follow artists, receiving notification whenever that artist publishes new works.

eBay Followed Search Feature (2013)

eBay is an online, consumer-to-consumer sales marketplace. Any search that a user performs on the platform can be made persistent by clicking the "Follow this search" feature. Users receive notifications when new matching items for sale are posted to the site.

Raymarine Evolution Autopilot (1984)

Raymarine produced the world's first digital cockpit autopilots in 1984. Modern systems like the Evolution Autopilot can take the helm for boat racing, easy cruising, or fishing.

ShotSpotter (1996)

ShotSpotter is a gunfire detection and location service. Working with police precincts, it monitors an array of microphones for gunfire. When it detects any, it triangulates the location and routes the information either to a dispatcher or directly to an officer to respond.

Kitestring (2002)

This personal safety agent lets users share their phone number, designate a person, prepare a message, and name a time. At the appointed time, Kitestring sends the user a text asking them if they're OK. If the user replies with a password, the event is forgotten. If there is no reply, or if the user replies with a panic password, then the message is sent to the designated person, who presumably uses the information in the message to track down the user and ensure their safety.

IBM Chef Watson (2014)

An instantiation of IBM's artificial intelligence Watson APIs, Chef Watson generates novel recipes based on existing recipes, an extensive database of related ingredients, and Eastern or Western taste profiles. Users can ask Chef Watson to be conservative with its recommendations or adventurous. A community of users shares results to discuss what worked and what didn't.

Narrative Clip (2012)

The hardware for this camera is an unassuming, plastic rounded-rectangle with a clip. As long as its lens detects light, it takes a photograph every 30 seconds. When reconnected to the internet, it uploads those photos to a server, which breaks them into scenes and then selects the best photo from each scene. It shares those back with the user who decides what to do with them, with easy tools for posting to social media.

iRobot Roomba Vacuum Cleaner (2002)

This large, puck-shaped vacuum cleaner leaves its charging station at times designated by its owner, and sweeps the floor in a pattern designed to provide maximum coverage and minimum overlap. When it is near to running out of battery life, it returns to the charging station.

Betterment Roboinvestor (2010)

Roboinvestors help investors name concrete financial goals, such as paying for college, meeting a monthly fixed income, or minimizing annual taxes. Thereafter, the agent manages investment portfolios to achieve (and hopefully outperform) the targets.

GOBI Library Solutions Collection Manager (c. 2000)

Patron-demand acquisition agents, like GOBI's, monitor the books that are borrowed from a library to infer topic trends and recommend new acquisitions as well as divestments to keep a collection relevant to its patrons' interests. (Be sure and read the Mr. McGregor section after Chapter 5 titled "About Chuck's Name" for a related warning about being too slavish to collections management software.)

Waze (2008)

Waze is a GPS-based navigation app with two agentive features of note. Like many navigation apps, Waze watches live traffic conditions to suggest when travelers should change routes. Additionally, Waze users can share their trips with people, who receive alerts of an estimated time for arrival when the trip is initially shared, anytime there is a significant change to that estimate, and minutes before the traveler is due to arrive.

IFTTT (If This Then That) (2010)

This service allows users to build persistent internet-based agents for a wide variety of devices and services.

NASA Remote Agent Architecture (1998)

Described in a paper titled "Remote Agent: To Boldly Go Where No AI System Has Gone Before," the Remote Agent is "specific autonomous agent architecture based on the principles of model-based programming, on-board deduction and search, and goal-directed closed-look commanding, that takes a significant step toward enabling [a future of space exploration via a heterogeneous fleet of robotic explorers]."

Chapter 5

Garden Defense Electronic Owl (2012)

This electronic scarecrow swivels the head of a plastic owl toward any movement it detects, with the intention of causing prey species to flee.

Chapter 8

Prospero: The Robot Farmer (2011)

Described by its inventor David Dorhout as an Autonomous Micro Planter, Prospero is a working prototype of a planting drone designed to work in swarms to plant seeds quickly, even in difficult terrain. Planned releases will use the drones to monitor crops and harvest them.

Volvo Self-Braking Trucks (2013)

Commercial trucks with this feature track and predict the movements of objects in their path. If the driver does not brake in time to avoid a collision, this agent applies the brakes itself.

Orbit Yard Enforcer (2012)

Similar to the Garden Defense Electronic Owl in concept, the Orbit Yard Enforcer is a lawn sprinkler that sprays water in response to any movement detected near it, with the intention of annoying garden and lawn pests so they flee.

Furuno NavPilot Autohelm (2011)

This autohelm is notable for the feature by which a captain can set a boat to perform repeating patterns of movement by selecting the pattern from a simple menu.

Chapter 11

Apple Time Machine (2007)

This agentive software makes backups of designated Mac OS hard drives. Users can rifle back through past states to restore the whole drive or individual files. Time Machine keeps more backups for more recent changes and automatically deletes the oldest backups to manage disk space.

Facebook Year in Review (2012)

This agentive content creator selects key images from a user's social media feed and renders them as components in a template video. The result is shared with users privately, who may then decide whether to dismiss it or share it with others. Similar content accompanies Facebook's Friendversaries and Friends Day events. Though these could be more customizable, users have the basic choice of whether to share them or not.

Chapter 12

Charlie (2016)

This agent keeps tabs on your calendar appointments and summarizes all the recent news relevant to the people you'll be meeting with, sending it to you a few hours ahead of time so you can queue up conversation topics.

INDEX

Bing, as search tool, 16
biometrics, as sensing technology, 76
blacklist, add to refine false positives, 123–124
boat autohelm agentive technology, 34–35, 129, 130–131, 205
Bostrom, Nick, 164, 185
bounty hunting, using agentive technology, 195
bow tie diagram, 71
Bradshaw, Jeffrey, 62
brain to tribe size ratio, 177
branding, in emergency situations, 146
Braue, David, 169
bribes, for service, 175
Burka, Daniel, 151
Butz, Albert, 7, 12, 200
bystander effect, in emergency handoff situations, 146

C

calendar appointment agent, Charlie, 177, 205
camera, Narrative Clip, 43, 44, 89, 169, 203
capability, conveyance in agent, 89–90, 97
Čapek, Karel, 56
card catalogs, 16
cars with autodrive. See self-driving cars
cat videos, 167–168
CD players, 15
channel, 127
Charlie app, calendar appointment agent, 177, 205
chatbots, 23
circadian rhythms, 166–167
cognitive biases, 48–49, 52
cognitive computing, 54
cognitive dissonance, 182
common sense engines, as thinking engineered into AI, 78
communications in space exploration, 51
community of practice, 192

completion, notifications when agent is running smoothly, 108
complexity
   agents' handling range of, 79–80
   of tasks, and trust in agent, 120
computer-supported cooperative work (CSCW), 54, 192
computers, ability to take initiative, 57
concern, notifications when agent is running smoothly, 110
confidence questions, in evaluation of agents, 153
confirmation bias, 182
constrained natural language builder
   looking under the hood, 94
   modifying linguistic rules, 132
   refining false positives, 125–127
constraints, explicit settings for agent setup, 93
conversational agents, 23–24, 28
conversational assistants, 24
conversational user interfaces, 23
cooperation, in evaluation of agents, 154
Copernicus, 183
corrective tools, 13, 16, 160
Cortana, 173–174
crime. See also ShotSpotter
   areas of, and agentive technology, 39
   from electric light technology, 166–167
   threats via bad actors, in agentive technology, 169–170
crutch, agents as, 163–164
customer service agents, 23, 174–175
customization, distributed, of new agent, 95
cybernetics, in history of agentive thinking, 54, 61

D

damper flapper, 7, 12, 200
DARPA robotic challenge, 63
Darwin, Charles, 184

M

N

ACKNOWLEDGMENTS

I owe a lot of thanks to people for helping to bring this book into being over the years.

Thanks to my publisher, Lou Rosenfeld, for believing in big ideas and my editor, Marta Justak, for trudging with me from the book proposal all the way to press.

Thanks to Steven Klocek, for prodding me into asking the biggest questions about our practice than I possibly could.

Thanks to design partners with whom I worked on projects that were agentive, but before we had a name for their category: Suzy Thompson, Jenea Hayes, and Dan Winterberg.

Thanks to others who worked with me through specific ideas over hang-outs, meals, and chats: Magnus Torstensson, Livia Sunesson, Amanda Peterson, John Langton, Michaël V. Dandrieux, and Gavin Jensen.

Thanks also to my technical reviewers for feedback on the first draft manuscript: Nir Eyal, Giles Colborne, Molly Wright Steenson, Jonathan Korman, Antti Oulasvirta, Matthew Milan, Mike Brand, Raphael Arar, and Cennydd Bowles. Your feedback kept me honest and on track.

Thanks to the organizations that took risks and invited me to speak about these ideas while they were still forming: RE:Design UX, Иннова, UX Conference and Sketchin, Øredev, Jawbone, Redshift Studio, IXDA, Normative, User Interface Engineering and the UX Virtual Symposium, UX Lisbon, UX Podcast, the Departure Unknown podcast, PRO Unlimited, the Institute for the Future, and APEX. It was through presentations and conversations that my stories got honed.

Thanks to every design pair who worked through "shufflers" and some version of the constrained natural language builder: Kim Goodwin, Lane Halley, and Doug LeMoine.

And thanks to the workshop attendees, audience members, and everyone else with whom I worked through these ideas, to punch them around and get them into shape for committing to a book. May history shine upon it favorably.

ABOUT THE AUTHOR

Christopher Noessel is a veteran of the interaction design industry, having designed products and services, and helped clients with design strategy across many disparate domains for more than 20 years. In that time, he co-founded a small interaction design agency where he developed interactive exhibitions and environments for museums. He worked as a director of information design at international web consultancy marchFIRST, where he also helped establish the interaction design Center of Excellence. For ten years, he worked with a boutique interaction design agency in San Francisco, where he led the "generator" half of that practice. He is now the Global Design Practice Manager for the Travel and Transportation industry at IBM, working closely with IBM Design. His desk, when he's at it, sits near the San Francisco home of Watson.

Christopher was one of the founding graduates of the now-passing-into-legend Interaction Design Institute Ivrea in Ivrea, Italy, where his thesis project was a comprehensive service design for lifelong learners called *Fresh*. The project was presented at the mLearn conference in London in 2003. He has since helped to visualize the future of counterterrorism as a freelancer, built prototypes of coming technologies for Microsoft, and designed telehealth devices to accommodate the crazy facts of modern health care.

Christopher has written for online publications for many years, but was first published in print as a coauthor of the interaction design pattern chapter in the textbook edited by Simson Garfinkel, *RFID: Applications, Security, and Privacy*. His Spidey sense goes off at random topics, and this has led him to speak at conferences around the world about a wide range of things, including interactive narrative, ethnographic user research, interaction design, pair design, sex-related interactive technologies, free-range learning, the future of tech, artificial intelligence, and the relationship between science fiction and interface design with the 2012 Rosenfeld Media book *Make It So: Interaction Design Lessons from Science Fiction*, coauthored with Nathan Shedroff. He is keeper of the blog scifiinterfaces.com and runs related sci-fi movie nights all over the world. In 2014, he coauthored the 4th

221

Edition of *About Face: The Essentials of Interaction Design*, helping modernize it for the six years that had passed since its prior release.

If you run into him on the street and want to get an earful, ask about any of the handful of other books he's got rattling around in his head. One involves the strange and wonderful world of generative randomness, and another involves the design of technology that helps its users get smart enough not to need it anymore.